Section Three — Themes

Section Four — Performance, Structure and Language

Section Five — Context and Critical Responses

Section Six — Writing About 'Hamlet'

Published by CGP

Editors:
Claire Boulter
Holly Corfield-Carr
Heather Gregson
Anthony Muller
Holly Poynton

With thanks to Luke von Kotze, Glenn Rogers, Elisabeth Sanderson and Paula Barnett
for the proofreading, and Laura Jakubowski and Laura Stoney for the copyright research.

Acknowledgements:

Cover Illustration by Daniela Illing - http://www.baerb.de

With thanks to iStockphoto.com for permission to use the image on page 1.

With thanks to Getty Images for permission to use the image on page 2.

Images on pages 3 and 36 from the Shakespeare's Globe Theatre production of Hamlet , photographers Fiona Moorhead & John Tramper

With thanks to Rex Features for permission to use the images on pages 3, 5, 16, 26, 28, 44, 50, 55, 56 and 61.

Images on pages 2, 3, 11 and 32 © CASTLE ROCK ENTERTAINMENT / THE KOBAL COLLECTION

Images on pages 3 and 38 © CASTLE ROCK ENTERTAINMENT / THE KOBAL COLLECTION / KONOW, ROLF

Images on pages 6, 8, 14, 18, 22, 30 and 34 © PARAMOUNT / THE KOBAL COLLECTION

Images on pages 12, 21 and 24 © CASTLE ROCK ENTERTAINMENT / THE KOBAL COLLECTION / MOUNTAIN, PETER

Image on page 75 © ODYSSEY / THE KOBAL COLLECTION

With thanks to The Moviestore Collection for permission to use the images on pages 3, 4 and 5.

With thanks to TopFoto for permission to use the images on pages 3, 40 and 46 © TopFoto

Page 1: Signature of William Shakespeare (1564-1616) (pen and ink on paper) Private Collection/ Ken Welsh/ The Bridgeman Art Library

Page 42: Frontispiece to 'The Spanish Tragedy' by Thomas Kyd (1558-94) printed by Augustine Mathewes, 1633 (woodcut) (b/w photo) by English School, (17th century) Private Collection/ The Bridgeman Art Library

Page 48: The Ambassadors, 1533 (oil on panel) by Holbein the Younger, Hans (1497/8-1543) National Gallery, London, UK/ The Bridgeman Art Library

Page 52: Stage and seating (photo) by Shakespeare's Globe, Southwark, London, UK/ © Peter Phipp/Travelshots/ The Bridgeman Art Library

Page 62: Portrait of Michel Eyquem de Montaigne (1533-92) (oil on canvas) by French School, (17th century) Private Collection/ Giraudon/ The Bridgeman Art Library

Page 64: Portrait of Dr. Samuel Johnson (1709-84) (oil on canvas) by Reynolds, Sir Joshua (1723-92) (after) Private Collection/ The Bridgeman Art Library

With thanks to Mary Evans Picture Library for permission to use the image on page 66.

Every effort has been made to locate copyright holders and obtain permission to reproduce sources.
For those sources where it has been difficult to trace the copyright holder of the work, we would be grateful
for information. If any copyright holder would like us to make an amendment to the acknowledgements,
please notify us and we will gladly update the book at the next reprint. Thank you.

ISBN: 978 1 84762 669 1
Website: www.cgpbooks.co.uk
Printed by Elanders Ltd, Newcastle upon Tyne.
Clipart from CorelDRAW®

Based on the classic CGP style created by Richard Parsons.

FOR

Advanced Level English

Hamlet

William Shakespeare

This book has everything you need to write a brilliant essay about *Hamlet*.
It's got a detailed scene-by-scene commentary as well as in-depth analysis
of the characters, themes, language techniques and critical context.

Plus, there are plenty of practice questions and tips
on how to improve your essays and bag those extra marks.

And of course, we've done our best to make the whole
experience at least vaguely entertaining for you.

The Text Guide

Contents

William Shakespeare and 'Hamlet'

*'Hamlet' is probably **Shakespeare's** most **Famous Play***

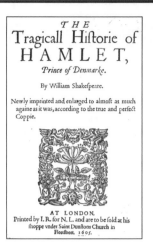

THE
Tragicall Hiſtorie of
HAMLET,
Prince of Denmarke.

By William Shakeſpeare.

Newly imprinted and enlarged to almoſt as much
againe as it was, according to the true and perfect
Coppie.

AT LONDON,
Printed by I. R. for N. L. and are to be ſold at his
ſhoppe vnder Saint Dunſtons Church in
Fleetſtreet. 1605.

1) *Hamlet* is a **play** about a **young prince** who wants to get **revenge** on his **uncle** for **murdering** his **father**.

2) It's always been **popular** — even in Shakespeare's **own lifetime** it was his **fourth most performed** play.

3) The reason for its **popularity** is that the themes of **love**, **betrayal**, **family**, **madness** and **revenge** are still **relevant** to audiences today.

4) It's also **popular** with **critics** because the **ideas** in the play can be **analysed** in many **different ways**.

*Shakespeare had a long **Dramatic Career***

© iStockphoto.com/Claudio Divizia

[signature]
1564 - 1616

- **April 1564** — **Born** in **Stratford-upon-Avon**
- **November 1582** — Aged 18, Shakespeare **marries Anne Hathaway**.
- **1583** — His daughter **Susanna** is born.
- **1585** — Has **twins**, **Hamnet**, a son, and **Judith**, a daughter.
- **Early 1590s** — Writes his **first plays**, *Richard III* and *Henry VI*, parts 1-3.
- **1594** — His **playing company** 'The **Lord Chamberlain's Men**' is **founded**.
- **1594 / 1595** — *Romeo and Juliet* is first **performed**.
- **1596** — His son **Hamnet dies**.
- **1599** — The **Globe Theatre** is **built**.
- **1600 / 1601** — *Hamlet* is first **performed**.
- **1603** — Writes *Othello*. 'The **Lord Chamberlain's Men**' change their name to 'The **King's Men**' when **James I** takes the **throne**.
- **April 1616** — **Dies** aged 52.

*Shakespeare was a **Man** of his **Era***

Religion

England was a **Protestant country**. **Christian morality** was **important**. → Many of Shakespeare's plays **deal with Christian beliefs**. His **villains** are often people who **give in** to a **deadly sin** e.g. greed, envy, wrath or gluttony.

Culture

England was going through a **cultural revival** known as the **Renaissance** (see p.62). The Renaissance **challenged traditional ideas** — Galileo proved that the Earth wasn't the **centre** of the **universe**, and **Machiavelli** (see p.28) **questioned** whether **politics** had to be **moral**. → Shakespeare also started to **challenge** traditional values. For example, he often used **figures of authority** as **fools**, and made **commoners** appear **intelligent**.

National Identity

English Renaissance culture focused on **national identity**. → **National identity** is a **theme** in a lot of Shakespeare's plays — he looks at **how countries develop** and **explores** the **relationship** between a **ruler** and their **country**.

Historical Background

Renaissance England Directly Influenced 'Hamlet'

1) The Renaissance encouraged people to **challenge everything** — that's why Hamlet spends so much time **questioning** the **world** around him.

2) A '**Renaissance Man**' was expected to have a knowledge of the **arts, philosophy** and the **sciences**. He would be a **deep thinker** who could **question** the world around him.

3) **Authors** and **playwrights** in the **Renaissance period** often **re-worked classic stories**. *Hamlet* is based on **two older works** — *Ur-Hamlet* and *Amleth* (see p.52).

4) The **Protestant Reformation** changed the way people at the time **thought** about **spiritual issues**. It placed massive importance on an **individual's conscience**. Everyone was **responsible** for their own **salvation** — this **troubles** Hamlet throughout the play.

'Hamlet' is Set in the Danish City of Elsinore

1) Shakespeare based Elsinore on a **real city** called **Helsingør**.

2) Almost all the scenes are set **inside Elsinore Castle** — this creates a **claustrophobic feeling** and suggests that Hamlet is **imprisoned** by the events in his life.

3) Elsinore had an **elective monarchy** — this meant that the **ruler** was **voted** in by the **nobility**. **Candidates** were usually from the **family** of the **dead monarch** — that's how **Claudius** took **power**.

4) Denmark was a **Protestant nation** — they didn't accept **Catholic ideas** and believed in **predestination**, the **idea** that God **controlled** everything that **happened**.

© CASTLE ROCK ENTERTAINMENT /THE KOBAL COLLECTION

'Hamlet' was Written for the Globe Theatre

This is what the **Globe theatre** might have **looked like**:

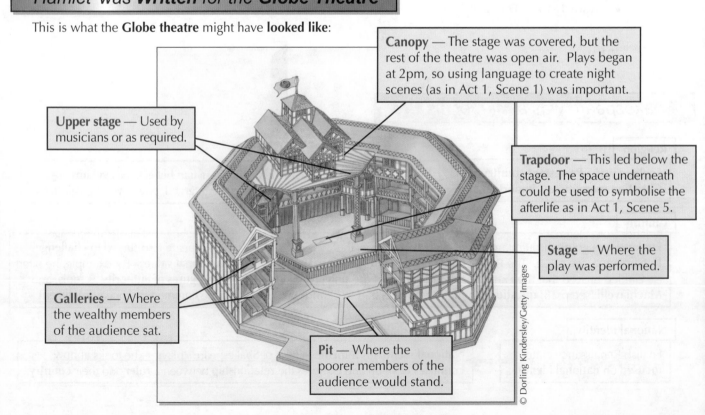

Canopy — The stage was covered, but the rest of the theatre was open air. Plays began at 2pm, so using language to create night scenes (as in Act 1, Scene 1) was important.

Upper stage — Used by musicians or as required.

Trapdoor — This led below the stage. The space underneath could be used to symbolise the afterlife as in Act 1, Scene 5.

Stage — Where the play was performed.

Galleries — Where the wealthy members of the audience sat.

Pit — Where the poorer members of the audience would stand.

© Dorling Kindersley/Getty Images

Who's Who in 'Hamlet'

The Danish Royal Family

Widowed — Married

The Ghost...
...claims to be Hamlet's dead father. He reveals that Claudius murdered him, and tells Hamlet to get revenge.

Gertrude...
...is Hamlet's mother. She marries Claudius after King Hamlet's death and relies on men to stay powerful.

Claudius...
...is Hamlet's uncle and the play's villain. He murdered his brother and married his wife so that he could become king.

Polonius's Family

Relationship

Hamlet...
...is the prince of Denmark and the play's hero. His quest for revenge is the main plot of the play.

Polonius...
...is Claudius's chief advisor. His constant scheming results in his death.

The Foreign Threat

Fortinbras...
...is a prince from Norway. He's a man of action who wants to reclaim his father's lands from Denmark.

Ophelia...
...is Polonius's daughter and Hamlet's love interest. She's controlled by the men in her life, and dies tragically.

Laertes...
...is Polonius's son and a foil to Hamlet. He's a man of action who kills Hamlet in revenge.

Other Courtly Characters

Horatio...
...is Hamlet's best friend — he's loyal and rational. He helps to explain the play's plot.

Rosencrantz & Guildenstern...
...are Hamlet's old school friends. They're interchangeable characters who betray Hamlet to help Claudius.

Play Synopsis

'Hamlet'... what happens when?

Here's a little recap of the <u>main events</u> in *Hamlet*. It's hard to remember what happens when, especially in a play that can take four hours to perform, so here's a handy guide so that you'll know roughly where to flick to. No need to thank us...

Act One — The Ghost Demands Revenge

> The **revenge plot** is introduced by the Ghost in Act 1, Scene 5.

© Moviestore Collection Ltd

- **Horatio** sees the **Ghost** of **King Hamlet** and worries that it represents a **threat** to **Denmark** — **Fortinbras**, a **Norwegian prince**, could be about to **invade**.
- **King Claudius** tells the court to **mourn** his **dead brother**, but also to **celebrate** his **marriage** to his brother's wife, **Gertrude**.
- Horatio tells **Hamlet** that he's seen the **Ghost** of his **father**.
- **Laertes** tells his sister **Ophelia** to **reject Hamlet**. Her father, **Polonius**, agrees. Laertes **leaves** for **Paris**.
- Hamlet **speaks** to his father's Ghost who **tells** him that he was **murdered** by Claudius. He asks Hamlet to **take revenge** on his uncle. Hamlet decides to **pretend** to be **mad**.

Act Two — Hamlet Pretends to be Mad

- Ophelia tells her father about Hamlet's **strange behaviour**. Polonius **believes** that Hamlet is **lovesick**.
- Claudius asks **Rosencrantz** and **Guildenstern** to **spy** on the prince.
- Polonius tells Claudius about his **suspicions** and they decide to **spy** on **Ophelia** and **Hamlet**.
- Hamlet **makes** Rosencrantz and Guildenstern **confess** that they're **working for Claudius**.
- A group of **players** arrive and Hamlet asks them to **perform** an **altered version** of the *Murder of Gonzago*. He thinks that the play's **similarities** to King Hamlet's **murder** will reveal Claudius's **guilt**.

Act Three — Polonius Spies on Hamlet

> The **revenge plot** is delayed when Hamlet **fails** to **kill** Claudius in Act 3, Scene 3.

- Claudius and Polonius **hide** and **wait** for Hamlet to meet Ophelia. Hamlet enters contemplating **suicide**.
- Hamlet reacts **angrily** to Ophelia and her **betrayal**. Claudius is **worried** by Hamlet's behaviour and **decides** to send him to **England**.
- Hamlet tells the players how to **act** his '**Mousetrap**' play. He **explains** the **plot** to the room as the players **perform**. Claudius calls for the play to **stop** and **leaves**.
- Claudius tries to **pray** and **admits** that he's guilty. Hamlet finds him praying but **doesn't kill him**.

© Moviestore Collection Ltd

- Hamlet **confronts** Gertrude for **betraying** his father, while Polonius **hides** behind an arras. Polonius calls for **help** but Hamlet **stabs** him, thinking that it's Claudius. When he **finds out** it's Polonius he decides to **hide the body**.
- The Ghost **re-appears** to **remind** Hamlet of his **quest**. Hamlet tells his mother that he's only **faking madness**, but **warns** her not to tell Claudius.

Act Four — *Hamlet's Exiled for Murdering Polonius*

- Gertrude tells Claudius that Hamlet is **mad** and has **killed** Polonius. Claudius is **scared** for his own **safety** and decides to send Hamlet away **as soon as possible**.
- Claudius sends Rosencrantz and Guildenstern to **find out** where Hamlet's **hidden** Polonius's body, but he **refuses** to tell them.
- Claudius tells Hamlet that he's sending him to **England** with Rosencrantz and Guildenstern. **Alone** on stage, Claudius **reveals** that he's sending Hamlet to his **death**.
- Hamlet **watches Fortinbras's army** march across Denmark and **compares himself** with the Norwegian prince. He decides that he should be **more like Fortinbras** and take **action**.
- Ophelia goes **mad** from **grief** and starts singing **songs**. **Laertes returns** to seek **revenge** for his father's **murder**.
- **Horatio** receives a **letter** from Hamlet, **explaining** that he's **escaped** from the **ship** and is **returning** to Denmark.
- Claudius tells Laertes that **Hamlet killed Polonius**. They **organise** a **fencing match** between Laertes and Hamlet, planning to use a **sharpened, poisoned sword** to **kill Hamlet**. Claudius **poisons** the **wine** in case Hamlet **wins**.
- Gertrude **announces** that Ophelia has **drowned**.

> Act 5, Scene 2 is the play's **dramatic climax** — Hamlet finally **acts** and takes **revenge**.

Act Five — *Hamlet Returns to Take his Revenge*

- Hamlet and Horatio **discuss death** with a **Gravedigger**.
- A **funeral procession** arrives in the **graveyard**, and Hamlet **discovers** that Ophelia has **died**. Hamlet **fights** with Laertes over who **loved** Ophelia **more**.
- After the funeral Hamlet **explains** to Horatio how he sent **Rosencrantz and Guildenstern** to their **deaths instead** of him.

- **Osric** tells Hamlet that he has been **challenged** to a fencing match with Laertes. Hamlet **agrees** to the contest.
- Hamlet **apologises** to Laertes and the contest **goes ahead**. During the fight Hamlet is **hurt** by the **poisoned sword**, but Laertes is also **stabbed** by the blade.
- Gertrude **toasts** Hamlet and **drinks** from the **poisoned wine**. As she dies she **exclaims** that the drink was poisoned. Laertes reveals that Claudius was **responsible**. Hamlet **stabs Claudius** with the **poisoned sword** and makes him **drink the wine**. Both Claudius and Laertes **die**.
- Before Hamlet **dies** he **tells Horatio** that Fortinbras should be the **next King**.
- Fortinbras **arrives** in Elsinore and finds **everyone dead**. He **takes** the **Danish throne**.

'Hamlet' — an incredibly complicated play...

As Shakespeare's longest play, *Hamlet* is jammed full of stuff — famous quotations, unanswered questions, thematic concerns... sounds a bit like an episode of *Lost*. Oh well — lucky for you, we've got another 72 pages in which to cover all the really important bits. Plus, there's a cartoon at the back of the book...

Act 1, Scene 1

The first scene takes place at night on the ramparts of Elsinore Castle. It's cold, dark, misty and foreboding...

The **Ghost Appears** to the **Guards**...

- **Bernardo** and **Marcellus** claim that they've seen the **Ghost** of the recently **dead king**, but **Horatio** is **sceptical**.
- The Ghost suddenly appears, but vanishes again. Horatio **agrees** that the Ghost does **look like** the dead king.
- Horatio **explains** that **Fortinbras** wants to **reclaim** lands that his father lost in a **battle** with **King Hamlet**.
- The Ghost reappears, but remains **silent** despite Horatio's **questions**. With dawn breaking, the Ghost disappears again. Horatio suggests that they tell **Prince Hamlet**, the dead king's son, about the Ghost.

Shakespeare uses various **language techniques** to create the right **mood** in this scene:

1) This scene **begins** with a question, "**Who's there?**" (line 1) and there are many more in the following **conversation**. This creates a **tense mood** of **uncertainty**.

2) Shakespeare also uses **half lines** to create a **broken rhythm** in the conversation. This increases the feeling of **uncertainty** and **unease** because the text doesn't **flow**.

3) The discussion about the Ghost is full of **contrasts** and **tensions**. Marcellus calls it "**majestical**" (line 144), but Horatio says that it acted "**like a guilty thing**" (line 149). This indicates that there's **confusion** over the Ghost's **intentions** and **origin** from the **start**.

The **Use** of the **Ghost Establishes** the **Genre**

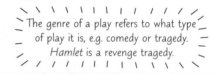
The genre of a play refers to what type of play it is, e.g. comedy or tragedy. *Hamlet* is a revenge tragedy.

© PARAMOUNT / THE KOBAL COLLECTION

1) The appearance of the Ghost means that the **audience** knows what to **expect** from the rest of the play. **Supernatural elements** were a **common theme** in **Elizabethan revenge tragedies** (see p.42).

2) The Ghost's existence indicates that "**Something is rotten in the state of Denmark**" (1.4.90). King Hamlet hasn't passed on to the afterlife **peacefully**, suggesting that there was something **suspicious** about his death.

3) The fact that the Ghost appears **wearing armour** also suggests that it's going to reveal an **aggressive message**.

4) The Ghost's appearance **foreshadows** the **tragedy** that's to come.

Horatio Introduces some **Key Themes**

1) Horatio helps the audience to understand what's happened:

- Horatio's **first thought** on seeing the Ghost is that Denmark's **future** under the new king is **uncertain**. He **voices** the **concerns** of the Danish people at a time of **political change**.
- He thinks the Ghost is a **bad omen** for Denmark. He compares it to the "**precurse of feared events**" (line 121) that **foreshadowed** the assassination of **Julius Caesar**, as portrayed in another Shakespearean play.
- Horatio is portrayed as **educated**, **rational** and **sceptical** — his **part-acceptance** of the Ghost's existence could **persuade** the **audience** to believe in the Ghost as well. Horatio's testimony is far more **convincing** than what the superstitious watchmen say.
- Shakespeare also gives Horatio the **capacity** to accept that he was **mistaken** when the Ghost **does appear**. However, he doesn't give up all his **scepticism** and maintains his **rational** views.

2) Once he's seen it, Horatio only **believes** "**in part**" (line 166) what the Ghost says — he's not **convinced**.

3) This develops the **theme** of **doubt** and **uncertainty** — the Ghost's **origin** and **motives** are **already** being **questioned**. This is **unusual** for a revenge tragedy so Shakespeare continues to **undermine** the audience's **expectations**.

Act 1, Scene 2

Scene 2 is set in the Great Hall of Elsinore Castle. It's bright, colourful, loud and is in stark contrast with Scene 1.

Claudius Addresses His Court...

- **King Claudius** speaks about his **brother's death**, his **marriage** to **Gertrude** and the threat of **Fortinbras's invasion**.
- Claudius sends ambassadors to **negotiate** with the King of Norway about Fortinbras and lets **Laertes** return to **France**.
- Both Claudius and Gertrude ask **Hamlet** to **stay** in **Denmark** and **criticise** his ongoing **grief**.
- Hamlet reveals that his **father's death** and his **mother's hasty marriage** has led him to **lose faith** in the **world**.
- **Horatio** tells Hamlet that he believes he has seen his father's **Ghost** — Hamlet agrees to keep **watch** with him.

Shakespeare sets up a **contrast** between the first two scenes:

1) The first scene has a **dark**, **foreboding atmosphere**, but in this scene Shakespeare introduces a **brightly lit** and **seemingly carefree** court — it's even introduced by a "*Flourish*" (fanfare).

2) This "*Flourish*" seems **inappropriate**, given that King Hamlet has only **recently died**. There's a sense that the court is **pretending** that everything's **normal** and is trying to **shake off** the **gloom** and **anxiety** that lay beyond the castle walls in **Scene 1**.

Shakespeare Reveals Claudius's Character

1) Shakespeare introduces Claudius as an **able king** (see p.29) but he **highlights** some major character **flaws**.

2) Claudius **convinces** the court to **accept** recent events by **juxtaposing** his brother's death with his marriage to Gertrude. However, his speech creates an **uncomfortable impression** — he uses **odd combinations** of words such as, "**defeated joy**" and "**mirth in funeral**" (lines 10–12) which don't **work together**.

3) Claudius's behaviour towards Hamlet is also **questionable** — he asks Hamlet to treat him like a **father**, saying that when he **dies**, Hamlet will be **king**. However, without his **intervention**, Hamlet would probably be king **already**.

4) The first scene **hints** at the widespread **concerns** that exist in Denmark, but this scene **reveals** exactly how "**rotten**" the state is. Claudius's **corruption** is a sign that Elsinore is **vulnerable**. Claudius admits that Fortinbras believes that "**by our late dear brother's death / Our state to be disjoint**" (lines 19–20).

Hamlet is Introduced as a Solitary Thinker

1) Shakespeare's **presentation** of Hamlet makes him **stand out**. **Only** Hamlet wears black **mourning clothes** of "**nighted colour**" (line 68), in visual **contrast** with the **colourful costumes** of the rest of the **court**. His **isolation** is made worse by the fact that **nobody else** appears **hostile** towards Claudius.

2) Gertrude even suggests that his mourning isn't **genuine**: "**Why seems it so particular with thee?**" (line 75). This **offends** Hamlet, who replies, "**I know not 'seems'**" (line 76) as he's the only person not **pretending** that **all is well**. He's either the only **honest** character at court, or the only one to **suspect** his uncle of **wrongdoing**.

3) Shakespeare reveals Hamlet's **thoughtful personality** through his **analysis** of grief (lines 76-86) and his **struggle** with the **morality** of suicide: "**O that this too too sullied flesh would melt**" (line 129). Hamlet's **loss of faith** in the **world** and the question of whether **suicide** can be **justified** are **major themes** throughout the rest of the play.

Practice Questions

Q1 Reread Act 1, Scene 1 and compare how the different characters in this scene describe the Ghost. Back up your answer with quotes from the text.

Q2 Reread Act 1, Scene 2 and assess how successful Claudius is in creating a positive mood within the court.

"Is not this something more than fantasy?"

It's probably helpful to follow this text analysis with an open copy of 'Hamlet' in front of you, that way you'll be able to see which bits fit in where. There's no denying that 'Hamlet' is a lengthy play, so make sure you stay hydrated and grab some high-energy snacks...

Act 1, Scene 3

Laertes is preparing to board the ship for France. Shakespeare delays the Ghost's return to build up the suspense...

Ophelia Gets Some Advice *from* Polonius *and* Laertes...

- **Laertes**, who's about to return to Paris, **advises Ophelia** not to carry on a **relationship** with **Hamlet**.
- **Polonius** gives Laertes some **advice** on **how to act** while he's away.
- After Laertes leaves, Polonius also speaks to Ophelia about the **dangers** of getting **involved** with Hamlet and tells her that she should **reject** his advances. Ophelia **agrees** to **obey** him.

Compared to Hamlet's **dysfunctional** family, Polonius appears to be the **head** of a more **conventional family**. Shakespeare uses this scene to draw more **contrasts** between **characters** in the play:

1) In the previous scene Hamlet rejects Claudius's and Gertrude's **advice** to **stop mourning**, but in this scene, Ophelia and Laertes seem to **accept** their **father's advice**: "**I shall obey, my lord**" (line 136).

2) Although a **lot** of Polonius's **patronising** advice is just a **thinly-veiled order**, there seems to be some genuine **fatherly love** behind it, which contrasts with Hamlet's **distant relationship** with his uncle.

3) This scene links to **Act 1**, **Scene 5**, where Hamlet's **conversation** with the **Ghost** is a **dark echo** of Polonius's father-son speech. However, **like Ophelia**, Hamlet **agrees** to his father's demands in spite of his **doubts** and says very **little**.

The Other Important Courtly Family *is* Introduced

Polonius *and* Laertes *are* Foils *to* Hamlet

> A foil is usually a character who contrasts with the protagonist (main character).

1) Shakespeare uses Polonius and Laertes as **foils** to develop **Hamlet's character**.

2) Polonius, Laertes and Hamlet all **love Ophelia**, and want to **protect her** — Polonius and Laertes want to protect her from **Hamlet**, and Hamlet wants to protect her from being **corrupted** by a **sinful world**.

3) Laertes has a **complicated relationship** with his sister. His use of **sexual imagery**, his **fixation** on her "**chaste treasure**" (line 31) and the **affectionate language** between them creates an **incestuous undertone**, which is similar to Hamlet and Gertrude's relationship (see p.31).

4) Polonius's **language** and **wordplay** are an **exaggerated version** of Hamlet's own **habits** (see p.35).

5) Laertes is a **rash**, a **man of action** and has inherited his father's **pompous** and **preachy attitude**. Shakespeare **hints** in this scene that Laertes's **action** is intended as a **foil** to Hamlet's **inaction** (see p.36).

Ophelia's Relationship *with* Hamlet *is a* Major Subplot

1) There are **three plots** in *Hamlet* — the **main revenge plot**, and **two subplots**. The first subplot involves the **threat of Fortinbras**, which is introduced in the first scene of the play. The second subplot revolves around **Hamlet and Ophelia's relationship**, which is introduced here.

2) Laertes **warns** Ophelia that Hamlet's **love** won't last, and Polonius fears that Hamlet is **untrustworthy**. Polonius **orders** Ophelia to **end** their relationship, which she **agrees** to. Ophelia's **rejection** probably **provokes** Hamlet's **cruel treatment** of her.

© PARAMOUNT / THE KOBAL COLLECTION

3) Both Polonius and Laertes act as though they have **complete authority** over Ophelia — like Hamlet, neither gives her much **credit**. Polonius thinks she's **foolish**, "**Pooh! You speak like a green girl**" (line 101) and Laertes suspects that she has **flawed judgment**, "**Youth to itself rebels, though none else near**" (line 44).

4) Ophelia doesn't reveal her **true feelings** in this scene, despite Laertes's and Polonius's **poor treatment** of her. This is a **theme** that **continues throughout** *Hamlet* — Ophelia only gets a voice when she goes **mad** (see p.68).

5) **Feminist critics** argue that Ophelia isn't as **developed** as the **male characters**. Unlike other Shakespearean **heroines** like Juliet from *Romeo and Juliet* or Viola from *Twelfth Night*, she just **gives in** to the **demands** of the **men** in her life.

Act 1, Scene 4

Back outside the castle once more, the atmosphere is just as dark, foreboding and mysterious as Scene 1...

The **Ghost Appears** to **Hamlet**...

- **Hamlet, Horatio** and **Marcellus** keep **watch** and wait for the **Ghost** to **reappear**.
- The group discuss the **state of Denmark** and the **behaviour** of the **new king** until the Ghost appears.
- The Ghost **beckons** Hamlet to **follow** it — Hamlet does, despite **warnings** from his **companions**.
- Marcellus and Horatio agree that something is **wrong** and decide to **follow** Hamlet and the Ghost.

This is a **short scene** but it has a number of **important purposes**:

1) It **mirrors** the **first scene** and builds up the **suspense** before the Ghost's appearance is **finally explained**.
2) In this scene, Shakespeare contrasts the **carefree court** with the **danger looming outside** the castle. The sound of the "*flourish of trumpets*" (between lines 6-7) **through** the castle walls shows that the **two worlds** are about to **collide**, and that the court can no longer **pretend** that **all is well**.
3) The **juxtaposition** of the old king's **torment** and the new king's **celebrations** within the castle is **ironic**. It seems as if the brothers' **fates** have been **inverted** — they've both got the **opposite** of what they **deserved**.

Shakespeare **Reveals** more about the **State** of **Denmark**

1) This scene develops the idea that Denmark is in a **poor condition** — the guards see the Ghost as a **sign** of **chaos**. Marcellus fears that "**Something is rotten in the state of Denmark**" (line 90).
2) Hamlet is still **hostile** towards Claudius, showing **disgust** for the tradition of **carousing**. Hamlet sees carousing as a **sign** of Denmark's **sinfulness**. Just as Denmark is **damaged** by a **reputation** for a particular sin (drunkenness), so a man's **positive qualities** can be **undermined** by a single **flaw**.

Carousing involves heavy drinking and behaving boisterously.

Shakespeare's Writing Technique
Hamlet's **view** that "**one defect**" (line 31) can **undermine** all of a man's **positive qualities** has been widely **analysed** by many **literary critics**, who see this as the **formula** for Shakespeare's **tragic heroes**. **Most** of Shakespeare's heroes, **including Hamlet**, have their otherwise **heroic qualities** undermined by a **single tragic flaw**.

Shakespeare **Develops** Hamlet's **Character Further**

1) This is the **final scene** before the **revenge plot** is introduced by the Ghost's **revelations**. Shakespeare uses it to show how Hamlet's **personality** will **shape** his pursuit of **vengeance**.
2) Hamlet already starts to **question** the Ghost's **uncertain origin** and **motives** (lines 40-42) — something that's on his mind for the **rest of the play**. However, Hamlet doesn't **fear** the Ghost because he's in such a **desperate state** that he **doesn't care** if he **lives** or **dies**: "**I do not set my life at a pin's fee**" (line 65).
3) Horatio introduces the **first doubts** about Hamlet's **sanity**, warning that the Ghost might "**draw [him] into madness**" (line 74). He worries that the Ghost could make Hamlet go **mad** by assuming a "**horrible form**" (line 72).
4) Hamlet puts his life in **destiny's** hands saying that "**My fate cries out**" (line 81), and Horatio also **declares** that "**Heaven will direct it**" (line 91). Shakespeare is telling the audience that Hamlet's **fate** is **inevitable** because he is a **tragic hero**. Once the revenge tragedy is set in **motion** in this scene, there's **no going back**.

Practice Questions

Q1 'Polonius is a good father to both Ophelia and Laertes.' To what extent do you agree with this statement?

Q2 Using Act 1, Scene 4 as a starting point, analyse how Shakespeare presents events which occur outside the castle.

"My father's spirit — in arms! All is not well"
Hamlet's dad goes into a bar... 'Sorry, we don't serve spirits here. We do a nice glass of revenge though. It's best served cold... but our fridge is on the blink, so it's lukewarm. It's not really your day is it sir? You could murder a Claudius? What's that, some kind of cocktail?'

Act 1, Scene 5

For the first and only time in the play, Hamlet and the Ghost are left alone on stage — the perfect time to reveal a few secrets...

The **Ghost Tells** Hamlet to **Seek Revenge**...

- The **Ghost** claims to be **Hamlet's father** and tells Hamlet to seek **revenge** for his murder.
- Hamlet's **suspicions** about **Claudius** are **confirmed** — his uncle seized the crown by murdering King Hamlet. The Ghost also tells Hamlet to leave **Gertrude alone**.
- Hamlet **agrees** to take revenge on Claudius, and the Ghost **disappears**.
- Hamlet tells his companions what **happened** and hatches a **plan** to pretend to be mad.

The **focus** of this scene is the **revenge plot**, but there are other important **dramatic features**:

1) *Hamlet* is one of Shakespeare's most 'self-conscious' plays — it frequently **refers** to the fact that it's a **play**. The line "**In this distracted globe**" (line 97) could mean that Hamlet is **close to madness**, or it could refer to the **Globe Theatre** where the play was **performed**.

When a play draws attention to the fact that it's a play, it's called metatheatre (see p.50).

2) The **interaction** between Hamlet and the Ghost **underneath the stage** can also be **interpreted** as an example of this **self-consciousness**. Hamlet uses a **playful tone** even though the scene is **serious**. Shakespeare could be drawing attention to the **dramatic limitations** of the theatre, **poking fun** at the fact that a ghost wouldn't be very **believable**.

The **Main Plot** of **Revenge** and **Madness** is **Introduced**

It's unusual for the **subplots** to be **introduced before** the main plot, but Shakespeare **challenged traditional conventions**. This scene establishes the main plot of **revenge** and **madness**:

Revenge

- The Ghost wants **retribution** — Claudius's sin must be **punished** to restore **justice**. Retributive justice has an **important role** in *Hamlet* — it **motivates** Hamlet, Laertes and Fortinbras. **Fear** of damnation is the main **cause** of Claudius's **guilt** (see p.16).

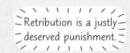
Retribution is a justly deserved punishment.

- Shakespeare **links** ideas of **justice** to **religion**. Hamlet describes the Ghost's order as a "**commandment**" (line 102), and the Ghost **compares** Claudius to **Satan**: "**a serpent stung me**" (line 36).
- However, the Ghost's demands for **revenge confuse** the **revenge plot**. His **ambiguity** provides Hamlet with the many **doubts** that **delay** his revenge (see p.41).

Madness

- The Ghost's appearance **causes** Hamlet to have a **spiritual dilemma** that **threatens** his sanity.
- Hamlet starts to **doubt his beliefs**. Hamlet's **faith** in humanity is already **shaken** by his mother's hasty marriage but in this scene he has to **rethink** his entire world view — the Ghost's uncertain origins and motives suggest to him that there are no **certain moral truths** even in the **afterlife**.
- Hamlet's **feigned madness** takes him very close to **real madness**. When the Ghost speaks from **under the stage**, Hamlet already **appears mad**, using **odd phrases**: "**Well said, old mole**" (line 162).

The **Ghost** is **Linked** to **Memory**

1) The Ghost addresses another **universal issue** — the **fear** of being **forgotten after death** (see p.41). The Ghost's **final request** to Hamlet is not **revenge**, but "**remember me**" (line 91), and Hamlet **repeats** this **three times** in his **soliloquy** (lines 92-112), confirming that he will "**remember**".

2) The Ghost fears that **Hamlet** will forget him, as **Gertrude** did. The Ghost has to remind Hamlet to take action **later** in the play, when he **forgets** about his **quest** in Act 3, Scene 4.

3) Shakespeare also **challenges** the **reliability of memory**. Hamlet remembers his father as "**Hyperion**" (1.2.140), but Hamlet has **idealised** his father. Human memory can't be **trusted** — Hamlet even has **difficulty** remembering **how long** his father's been **dead** (1.2.138).

Hyperion was the Greek god of the sun.

Act 2, Scene 1

A few weeks have passed since Hamlet's encounter with the Ghost, but not much has changed...

Hamlet **Begins** to **Act Mad**...

- **Polonius** sends his servant **Reynaldo** to **spy** on **Laertes** and **report** back on his son's **behaviour**.
- Soon after Reynaldo leaves, **Ophelia** enters, looking very **upset**. She tells Polonius about a visit from **Hamlet** in her **closet**. She describes his **appearance** as **dishevelled**, and says that he seemed **mad**.
- Polonius takes this **behaviour** as a **sign** of Hamlet's **love** for Ophelia and decides to **tell Claudius**.

The first part of the scene **develops** Polonius's **character** and the second part furthers the **Hamlet** and **Ophelia subplot**.

Shakespeare **Develops** the **Unpleasant Side** of Polonius

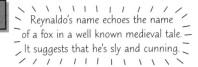
Reynaldo's name echoes the name of a fox in a well known medieval tale. It suggests that he's sly and cunning.

Polonius can be **interpreted** as either a **blundering fool** or a **cunning manipulator**. This scene provides **good evidence** for **both** (see p.34):

1) His **instructions** to **Reynaldo** show that he's a **devious schemer** — his **suggestions** about **how** to **get information** about Laertes are **intelligent**, even if they aren't particularly **moral** (lines 6-68).

2) The idea that **language** can be **manipulated** to shape the **truth** is a **major theme** in *Hamlet*. Polonius tells Reynaldo to use words to **"breathe his faults so quaintly / That they may seem the taints of liberty"** (lines 31-32).

3) However, Polonius's **cunning** is undermined when he **muddles** his words and **loses the thread** of the conversation: **"What was I about to say? By the mass, I was about to say something! Where did I leave?"** (lines 49-51).

4) **Coleridge** suggests that Polonius used to be a **cunning politician**, but has become a **buffoon** in his **old age** — in this scene he's **"the skeleton of his own former skill and statecraft"**. Whether Polonius is a **fool** or a **manipulator**, it's clear that **deception** is **common** in Claudius's **corrupt court**.

Ophelia and Hamlet's **Relationship** gets **Complicated**

1) Polonius's conversation with Ophelia has several **narrative functions**:

- It reveals that Hamlet has already begun to **feign madness**.
- It shows that Ophelia has **followed** Polonius's **orders** and **rejected Hamlet**.
- It sparks off Polonius's **belief** that Hamlet's **madness** is caused by **love**.

2) Ophelia's **apparent rejection** of Hamlet could confirm her **obedience**, but the closet scene happens **offstage** so it's **unclear** whether her **chastity's** actually intact (see p.33).

3) The fact that this closet scene occurs **offstage** also means that the **audience** doesn't know whether Hamlet was **really mad** or just **acting**.

4) If Hamlet is **faking madness**, it seems as if he's just **using Ophelia**, knowing that she'll tell Polonius who will **report** back to Claudius. However, he might be **genuinely upset** about the breakdown of their relationship.

5) **Feminist critics** have used this scene as further **evidence** that Ophelia has **no voice** (see p.68). They argue that she's just used as a **pawn** by the **men** in her life, to do as they **"command"** (line 108).

Practice Questions

Q1 'Shakespeare's frequent reference to the workings of the theatre reduces the impact of *Hamlet* on the audience.' To what extent do you agree with this statement? Refer to the text in your answer.

Q2 Using Act 2, Scene 1 as a starting point, analyse why Shakespeare chose to have some events occur offstage in *Hamlet*.

"O day and night, but this is wondrous strange"

Act 1, Scene 5 reaffirms that Horatio is like the chorus — his assertion that the Ghost is an omen of trouble is proved right. The audience knows they can trust anything he says, even if he asks you to jump off a bridge. Ophelia took this a bit too literally...

Act 2, Scene 2

By far the longest scene in 'Hamlet', Act 2, Scene 2 is crammed full of revelations and important themes...

Hamlet **Plans** to **Prove** Claudius's **Guilt** with a **Play Within** the **Play**...

- **Claudius** has summoned **Rosencrantz** and **Guildenstern**, old **school friends** of **Hamlet's**, to court so that they can **spy** on the prince and work out why he's been **behaving so strangely**.
- The **ambassadors return** from **Norway** and report that **Fortinbras** is going to **invade Poland** instead of **Denmark**.
- **Polonius** tells **Gertrude** and **Claudius** that he **suspects** Hamlet's behaviour is caused by **lovesickness**.
- Polonius suggests that they **spy** on Hamlet and use **Ophelia** to test his **theory**. Claudius and Gertrude **agree**.
- Hamlet meets Polonius, and then Rosencrantz and Guildenstern, and **mocks** them all.
- Rosencrantz and Guildenstern introduce the **travelling players** and Hamlet asks them to **perform** his **play**.

There are **four main parts** to this scene:

1) Claudius, Gertrude and Polonius **discuss** Hamlet's **state of mind** and how to **deal** with it.
2) Hamlet **appears on stage** for the **first time** since his decision to **fake madness**, and starts to **mock** Polonius.
3) Hamlet **meets** with Rosencrantz and Guildenstern and they **admit** that they're **working** for Claudius.
4) Hamlet **meets** the **players** and **decides** to use them in a **plan** to **reveal** Claudius's **guilt**.

These parts all take place in the **same location** and happen **straight after each other**.
This creates a sense of claustrophobia and makes it seem as if "**Denmark's a prison**" (line 243).

Deception is Widespread in Claudius's Court

1) **Polonius used** Reynaldo to spy on Laertes in the **previous scene** — this **anticipates Claudius's plans** to use Rosencrantz and Guildenstern to spy on Hamlet.

2) Rosencrantz and Guildenstern are **interchangeable** — they're basically **doubles** of each another. This highlights the **duplicity** which is **widespread** in Claudius's court (see p.39).

   > Duplicity can mean 'deceitful', but it can also mean 'two of something'.

3) Rather than **confronting** Hamlet himself, Claudius uses Hamlet's friends to find out the truth, before **agreeing** to Polonius's **plan** to **spy** on the prince.

4) **Ironically**, Claudius calls Polonius "**faithful and honourable**" (line 130), despite his **scheming ways**, and he seems to **admire** Polonius's **willingness** to use his **own daughter** as part of his deception.

There's **Humour** in Hamlet's **Madness**

1) Hamlet's **apparent madness** lets him **mock** Polonius without trying to hide it. Even before Hamlet enters, Gertrude criticises Polonius for **droning on, vainly trying** to make him get to the **point**. She demands "**More matter, with less art**" (line 95).

   > This line could describe *Hamlet* itself — Shakespeare might be poking fun at his contemporary critics.

2) Hamlet follows his mother's lead, also **mocking** Polonius's **foolishness**:

   - He uses **words** that have **multiple meanings** to **confuse** Polonius. Hamlet calls him a "**fishmonger**" (line 174), accusing him of **prostituting Ophelia** and using her as **bait** (see p.34). Polonius **thinks** he's **talking nonsense**.

   - He uses **gibberish** to **insult** him — he says that Ophelia might **breed** like **maggots** in a **dead dog** (lines 181-186) but it goes over Polonius's head.

   - Ironically, whenever Hamlet's speaking **nonsense**, Polonius thinks that he makes a lot of **sense** — he says that Hamlet speaks a "**happiness that often madness hits on, which reason and sanity could not**" (lines 209-211).

3) Hamlet also **mocks** Rosencrantz and Guildenstern's **stupidity** by giving **ridiculous answers** they can't **understand**.

4) Hamlet's use of **dark humour** in this scene has also been used as **evidence** of his **sanity** (see p.27).

Act 2, Scene 2

The Audience Witnesses Hamlet's Madness

1) This is the **first time** that the audience **sees** Hamlet's **'madness'**, and it's very **convincing**. **Weeks** have passed since Hamlet saw the Ghost, so it's **impossible** to say whether he's been drawn "**into madness**" (1.4.74) by seeing it.

2) Hamlet's **grief** and Ophelia's **recent rejection** could have made him mad. Ophelia's **description** of Hamlet's **appearance** with "**doublet all unbraced, / No hat upon his head, his stockings fouled**" (2.1.78-79) suggests **real madness**. Playwrights **commonly** used **dishevelled clothes** as a **visual sign** that a character had gone **mad**.

3) However, Hamlet's **witty language** suggests that he's only **pretending**. He says that he's only mad occasionally: "**I am but mad north-north-west**" (line 377). This suggests that he can **choose** to be **mad** or **sane**.

4) Claudius is more **worried** about the **threat** posed by Hamlet's **madness** than the potential threat posed by Fortinbras's **army**. In **contrast** King Hamlet was more **concerned** with **foreign military threats**.

The Players Have an Important Role

> Despite Hamlet's morals, he takes a leaf out of Claudius's book by using deception (the play within a play) for his own purposes.

1) The **players** in *Hamlet* have an important **dramatic function** — they **inspire** Hamlet's **plan** to uncover Claudius's guilt. They also allow **Shakespeare** to **comment** on the **theatre**:

- Rosencrantz's description of **child actors** as "**little eyases**" (line 338) or 'little hawks' is a **criticism** of the '**children only**' theatre companies — an ongoing **theatrical conflict** which Shakespeare was **aware** of.
- Shakespeare gives Hamlet an **appreciation** of plays to **criticise those** who didn't **appreciate good writing**. Hamlet says that he remembers a play that "**pleased not the million**" (line 435), but he **enjoyed** it.

2) Shakespeare goes on to **examine** whether **acting** can provoke **genuine emotion**:

- Hamlet's impressed by a player's convincing **emotional response** to "**a fiction... a dream of passion**" (line 549).
- Shakespeare once more **draws attention** to the **fact** that *Hamlet* is a piece of **fiction** itself. He's also **highlighting** the **irony** that the **audience** is about to **watch** a **play within the play**.

> **Contemporary Commentary**
>
> Rosencrantz says the players are **travelling** because of some recent "**inhibition**" (line 331). This could be a **reference** to the **unsuccessful Essex Rebellion** of 1601 — **public theatres** were often **shut down** during times of **unrest**.

Hamlet Curses his Lack of Action

1) Hamlet's **impressed** that the player can "**force his soul**" (line 550) to show emotion for **characters** and **stories** that mean "**nothing**" to him (line 554). He calls himself a "**coward**" (line 568) for not dealing with his own **very real** concerns. His **fury** and feelings of **inadequacy** force him to act, by deciding to **prove** Claudius's **guilt** with a **play**.

2) Even though **Fortinbras** has been persuaded **not to invade** Denmark, **unlike Hamlet**, he doesn't sit around **moping**. Instead he **pursues war** in **Poland** and kills **innocent men** over a tiny piece of **land**. In **Act 4, Scene 4**, Hamlet **compares himself** with Fortinbras and finally **realises** that he must **act**.

Practice Questions

Q1 'Act 2, Scene 2 is the key turning point in *Hamlet*.'
To what extent do you agree with this assessment? Back up your answer with examples from the text.

Q2 Using Act 2, Scene 2 as a starting point, analyse the importance of deception in *Hamlet*.

"The play's the thing / Wherein I'll catch the conscience of the King"

Sometimes I think Hamlet's a bit annoying. Prancing around like he's better than everyone else. 'Oooo look how intelligent I am, I'm just soooo funny, oh boo hoo, my uncle is just the meanest!' Thank goodness he dies at the end. He ain't so clever now...

Act 3, Scene 1

This scene is full of yet more deception, but the highlight is Hamlet's soliloquy — "To be, or not to be..."

Claudius and Polonius Spy on Hamlet...

- **Rosencrantz** and **Guildenstern** tell **Claudius** that they **don't know** what's **caused Hamlet's madness**.
- Claudius **acknowledges** his **guilty conscience** to the audience for the **first time** in the play.
- Hamlet again considers the **morality** of **suicide** in his **soliloquy** — "**To be, or not to be**" (line 56).
- **Polonius** and Claudius **eavesdrop** on Hamlet's **meeting** with **Ophelia**. Hamlet reacts **angrily** to her and appears to be **mad**. Claudius decides to **send him away**.

This scene has **severe consequences** for Hamlet:

1) Hamlet's **ramblings** to Ophelia in this scene **convince** Polonius that the prince is **lovesick**, but Claudius **disagrees**. Polonius **persuades** Claudius to arrange a **meeting** between Gertrude and Hamlet in Gertrude's **closet** so that he can **eavesdrop** and **prove** his **theory** (Act 3, Scene 4).

2) This meeting proves to be both Polonius's and Hamlet's **downfall**. Hamlet **accidentally kills** the "**intruding fool**" (3.4.32), which in turn **motivates Laertes** to **return** to Elsinore and seek **revenge** on Hamlet.

3) This scene also **illustrates** Claudius's **fear** of Hamlet — he says that "**There's something in his soul**" (line 165) which could be dangerous, and so he **decides** to send Hamlet to **England**.

© PARAMOUNT / THE KOBAL COLLECTION

Hamlet's soliloquy is strangely fluent and has a steady tone and tempo — it lacks the passion of someone wrestling with such intense feelings and problems.

Hamlet has a Soliloquy About Suicide

1) In Hamlet's **soliloquy**, he **discusses suicide** but he never refers to himself when talking about it. This suggests that he's only **considering** suicide as a **philosophical idea** in general.

2) It sounds as if he's posing a **hypothetical argument** with an **imaginary listener**, rather than **actually considering** taking his own life. Hamlet's **Christian morals prevent** him from committing suicide, but that doesn't stop him from **considering** the **issue**.

3) He argues that life is so **miserable** and "**weary**" (line 77) that suicide would **appeal** to **most people**, if it wasn't for the **uncertainty** of the **afterlife**. Hamlet suggests that mankind would "**rather bear those ills we have / Than fly to others that we know not of**" (lines 81-82).

Hamlet Uses Ophelia as an Outlet for his Anger

1) Hamlet reacts **furiously** to Ophelia in this scene. He seems **disgusted** by women:

- He **denies** that he ever loved her and tells her "**Get thee to a nunnery**" (line 121). This line is **ambiguous** (see p.32) but the **most common interpretation** is that Hamlet wants to **save Ophelia** from becoming a "**breeder of sinners**" (line 122). He barely thinks any better of men, calling them "**arrant knaves**" (line 129).

- He **criticises all women**, calling them **dishonest** (a pun on the fact that 'honest' also means '**chaste**') for making their faces "**paintings**" (line 143) and turning men into "**monsters**" i.e. 'cuckolds' (line 139). Hamlet means that women make themselves look **beautiful** and "**jig and amble**" (line 145) to get **husbands**, but then they **betray** them.

2) Ophelia finally voices her **true feelings** for Hamlet in this scene as she **sadly mourns** the "**noble mind**" that has been "**o'erthrown**" by madness (line 151).

3) The **audience knows** that they're being **watched**, but it's **unclear** if Hamlet **knows** this — his **cruelty** to Ophelia seems to suggest that he does **know**. If Hamlet does know, and his **furious treatment** of Ophelia is just an **act** for the **observers**, it's a **failure** — it doesn't **convince Claudius** that he's **truly mad**.

Ironically it's Ophelia's eavesdropping father who's dishonest — he even says that "pious action" is a good cover for wicked deeds (lines 48-49).

Act 3, Scene 2

In a makeshift theatre the players get ready to perform for the royal family...

Hamlet's **Play** is **Performed For Claudius**...

Hamlet's play is based on 'The Murder of Gonzago' but he tells Claudius it's called 'The Mousetrap' (line 247) as he's using it to trap Claudius.

- **Hamlet directs** the players how to **act** to make the **best impact**.
- Hamlet **continues** to **taunt Ophelia**, making **sexual jokes** at her **expense**.
- The play is **performed**, with Hamlet providing a **commentary** on the play's events.
- When Claudius **recognises** a **similarity** between the **play** and his **own actions** he calls for it to **stop**. Hamlet thinks the play has been a **success**.
- **Rosencrantz** and **Guildenstern** enter and tell Hamlet that **Gertrude** wants to see him. Hamlet **bitterly criticises** his two old friends for their **betrayal**.

In this scene it's Hamlet's turn to try to **catch** Claudius out:

1) Hamlet believes that the play is a chance to prove the Ghost's **accusations**. In the play, **Gonzago's nephew murders** him and **marries** his wife, **Baptista**.

2) Although Hamlet **believes** the play's a **success**, Horatio **doesn't** seem so **sure** (line 288). Claudius's **reaction** to the play could simply be because he's **afraid** that his nephew has **murderous desires** (like the **plot** of '**The Mousetrap**').

There are multiple layers of observation in this scene — the audience is watching Hamlet, who is watching Claudius and Gertrude, who are watching the play.

Hamlet's **Relationships** are **Developed**

1 Horatio

- Hamlet **admires** the fact that Horatio is "**not passion's slave**" (line 82). Hamlet wears him in his "**heart's core**" (line 83).
- Hamlet also **praises** Horatio for his **self-control** and the fact that he's "**not a pipe for Fortune's finger**" (line 80).
- His conversations with Horatio are **sane** and **coherent** — Hamlet **trusts** him enough to let him be a part of his **plan**.

2 Gertrude

- Hamlet **refuses** his mother's **request** to sit by her, and instead sits by Ophelia, saying she's "**more attractive**" (line 119).
- Although the play is **mainly used** as a **trap** for **Claudius**, it also **criticises** Gertrude. In the first scene, the Queen **repeatedly promises** her husband that she'll **never remarry**.
- Gertrude says "**The lady doth protest too much, methinks**" (line 240) but Hamlet **replies** that the play shouldn't bother "**free souls**" with **clean consciences** (line 251).
- Hamlet realises that he must **confront** her, but also **control** his anger: "**I will speak daggers to her, but use none**" (line 403).

3 Ophelia

- Hamlet makes **crude comments** to **test** Ophelia's **honesty** by seeing how she **reacts**.
- He asks Ophelia "**Lady, shall I lie in your lap?**" (line 121) and then **questions** whether Ophelia **interprets** this **sexually**.
- Hamlet's **sarcastic mocking** and **contempt** for **Ophelia** anticipates the **anger** that he unleashes on **Gertrude** in Act 3, Scene 4.

4 Rosencrantz & Guildenstern

- Hamlet **manipulates** Rosencrantz and Guildenstern and **attacks** them for their **dishonesty**.
- He initially appears **disappointed** by his friends' **betrayal**, but soon launches into a **verbal attack**. When Guildenstern **refuses** to play the recorder, Hamlet **angrily** points out that "**You would play upon me**" (lines 372).

Practice Questions

Q1 Reread Hamlet's soliloquy in Act 3, Scene 1, lines 56-88 and rewrite it in modern English.

Q2 'Ophelia should be viewed as a completely innocent victim.'
Using Act 3, Scene 2 as a starting point, write an argument both for and against this statement.

"To be, or not to be — that is the question"

Essentially, Hamlet's asking if he should live or die. Live or die? Live or die? Tough call in anyone's book. Unless that book is Bram Stoker's 'Dracula' — Live or die OR living dead? A much easier decision. Always go for undead — it's the best of both worlds.

Act 3, Scene 3

This scene possibly takes place in a chapel — it's Hamlet's first real opportunity to kill Claudius...

Claudius Prays to God...

- **Claudius** is **worried** by **Hamlet's** 'Mousetrap' play and decides to send Hamlet **away** to **England** as soon as possible. He asks **Rosencrantz** and **Guildenstern** to **go with** the prince.
- Once he's left **alone**, Claudius **prays** to God in the **vain hope** that he might be **forgiven** for his **sins**.
- Hamlet **finds** Claudius **praying**, but decides **not to kill** him as he's **worried** that his **soul** would go to **Heaven**.

This scene **reveals** a lot about **Claudius's character**:

1) Claudius has **surrounded** himself with people like Polonius who just say what he wants to hear: "**as you said, and wisely was it said**" (line 30). Rosencrantz flatters Claudius saying that he's more **important** than the "**lesser things**" (line 19) like the **Danish people**.

2) In this scene Claudius **speaks** in a **similar way** to Hamlet, asking **rhetorical questions** as if he's **discussing** his problems with an **unseen listener**. Claudius's speech is also **rational** and **ordered**. This shows how **intellectually similar**, but **morally different** Hamlet and Claudius are.

In the Bible, Cain and Abel are Adam and Eve's sons — Cain kills his brother, Abel.

Claudius isn't Genuinely Repentant

1) Claudius is **sceptical** that **prayer** will **help** him, because he's committed the crime that **God himself condemned** when Cain killed Abel: "**It hath the primal eldest curse upon't**" (line 37).

2) Claudius's prayers are **motivated** by **fear** and **guilt**, but not **genuine repentance**: "**My words fly up, my thoughts remain below. / Words without thoughts never to heaven go**" (lines 97-98).

3) Claudius can't **repent** because he's **selfish** and **unwilling** to give up what he's **gained** from King Hamlet's **murder**: "**May one be pardoned and retain th'offence?**" (line 56).

4) Claudius knows that he'll have to face **punishment** for his **sins** in the **afterlife**. This **indicates** that Claudius **exists** in the same **Christian world** as Hamlet and there must be **moral justice**.

5) Claudius's **doubts** about praying are **justified** because without **genuine repentance**, he can never be **forgiven**. Ironically his **prayers save** him, not from **God's judgement**, but from **Hamlet's sword**.

Hamlet's Refusal to Kill Claudius is Confusing...

1) Hamlet's lack of action in this scene has caused a lot of **critical debate** because it raises a lot of **questions**.

2) Hamlet says that he doesn't want to kill Claudius **in prayer** in case his uncle "**goes to heaven**" (line 74). Many critics argue that Hamlet's refusal to kill Claudius isn't **fully explained**. There are other **potential explanations** for his **delay**:

- **Plot device** — The fact that Claudius **admits** his **guilt** in this scene and Hamlet seems **ready** to take **revenge** suggests that this is the play's **conclusion**. However, Shakespeare is just **challenging** the audience's **expectations** and building **suspense**.
- **Tragic flaw** — Hamlet is **unable** to act given the opportunity. He gives **unnecessarily complex** reasons to **justify** more **procrastination**.
- **Conscience** — Despite Claudius's **guilt**, Hamlet doesn't want to **kill** in **cold blood**. His **reasoning** could just be a way to avoid **committing murder**.
- **Fairness** — Hamlet wants to **murder** his uncle in the **same state** as his father. He believes that his father's soul was **unclean** at the time of his death, but he isn't **certain**: "**who knows save heaven?**" (line 82). He's **uncertain** about whether murdering Claudius in prayer would be '**fair**' so **refuses** to do it.

© Donald Cooper/Rex Features

Act 3, Scene 4

This scene takes place in Gertrude's closet. A closet wasn't necessarily a bedroom — it was more like a private chamber.

Hamlet is **Angry** with **Gertrude**...

- **Polonius** tells **Gertrude** what to **say** to **Hamlet**. He then **hides** behind an **arras** (tapestry).
- Hamlet **confronts** his mother and hears Polonius call for **help**. He assumes it's **Claudius** and **kills him**. Realising his **mistake**, Hamlet continues to **criticise** Gertrude for her **betrayal** of his father.
- The **Ghost reappears** and **reminds** Hamlet of his **purpose**. He tells Hamlet to be **kind** to Gertrude.
- Hamlet **reveals** to Gertrude that he's only **pretending** to be **mad** and she **agrees** to keep it **secret**.

1) This is the **only time** in the play that Gertrude and Hamlet are **alone**. In many ways it **echoes** the earlier 'nunnery episode'. Gertrude talks to Hamlet in **unnatural language** which makes her seem **cold** and **distant**.

2) Gertrude isn't as **quick-witted** as her son — she tries to **tell Hamlet off**, but he **seizes control** of the **conversation**. He **mocks** her by **twisting** her **words** and **repeating** them back to her in the **same rhythm**. This **inverts** the traditional **parent-child relationship**.

Hamlet **Finally Confronts** his **Mother**

This scene gives the most **revealing insights** into Gertrude's **character,** even though she only gives **brief responses** to Hamlet's **verbal attack**. Hamlet's **confrontation** could have several **motives** — he could want to:

Confirm Claudius's Guilt	• Hamlet wants to **find out** if Gertrude **knew** about Claudius's **crime**, or whether she was **involved**. • She appears **naive** — her **shocked echo** of Hamlet's **accusation** (line 31) and the **wringing** of her **hands** (line 35) suggests that she was **innocent** of King Hamlet's **murder** and **unaware** of it.
Make Gertrude Repent	• Hamlet wants to make Gertrude **aware** of her **sins** and **save her soul** — critics have argued that Hamlet is more **committed** to this than carrying out his **revenge**: he's "**cruel only to be kind**" (line 179). • His **language** is **similar** to a **preacher**, using words like "**grace**", "**judgement**" and "**hell**" (lines 42, 71 & 83).
Repair their Relationship	• Hamlet seems **very upset** by his mother's **rejection** — his **hatred** of Claudius (even **before** the Ghost appears) could be partly because he's **replaced** Hamlet in Gertrude's **affections**. • However, the scene **concludes** with a **veiled threat**: "**break your own neck down**" (line 197). Hamlet's not willing to **sacrifice** his quest for **revenge** in favour of **repairing** their **relationship**.

Polonius's Murder is out of **Character** for **Hamlet**

1) The **murder** of Polonius undermines Hamlet's **role** as a **moral hero**. The murder is **unjustified**, and he's not concerned about the **consequences** — this calls Hamlet's **morality** into **question**.

2) Hamlet's **spontaneous reaction** contrasts with his **hesitation** over killing Claudius in the **previous scene**. It's an example of Hamlet being unable to **coordinate** his **thoughts** and **actions**. In this scene he proves that **impulsiveness** isn't the **answer** either. The **wrong man** is killed and Hamlet seals his **own fate**.

3) Polonius's murder is the **main incident** in the play that **shows** that Hamlet might be **genuinely mad** — it's a **completely uncontrolled impulse** without any **logic** behind it. Hamlet believes that **Claudius** was **behind** the arras but that would have been **impossible** as Hamlet had only just left him praying.

Practice Questions

Q1 Analyse Hamlet's soliloquy in Act 3, Scene 3, lines 73-96 and decide the most probable reason for Hamlet's hesitation.

Q2 'Act 3, Scene 4 proves that Gertrude is just an innocent victim.' To what extent do you agree with this statement?

"Almost as bad... As kill a king and marry with his brother"

If this was a film, I'd be shouting at the screen, 'Oh for heaven's sake, just kill him already!' But they never do, and it always comes back to haunt them later. Thinking about it, Claudius did kill King Hamlet already, but he came back to haunt him anyway. You can't win...

Act 4, Scenes 1-2

Act 4 is a series of fast moving events. This is typical of revenge tragedies but seems odd in a play full of delays...

Act 4, Scene 1 — Gertrude and Claudius Lie to Each Other...

- **Gertrude** speaks to **Claudius** — she tells him that **Hamlet** is **mad** and has **killed Polonius**.
- Claudius asks **Rosencrantz** and **Guildenstern** to **find out** where Hamlet has **hidden** the **body**.

1) Gertrude's **anxiety links** this scene with the previous one and **joins** the **two acts**.

2) Claudius asks Gertrude to "**translate**" (line 2) her sobs, but Shakespeare **highlights** Gertrude's **submissiveness** as she simply **answers** Claudius's **questions** rather than **speaking freely**. As a result, Gertrude's **true character**, **thoughts** and **feelings** remain **hidden**, like Ophelia's.

3) Both Claudius and Gertrude have just been through **traumatic events**, but they make little effort to comfort each other. Their conversation is full of **lies**, and their relationship is **distant**.

4) Gertrude and Claudius **are**:

SELF-CENTRED	1) Gertrude **immediately reports** back to Claudius, instead of keeping what **happened** with Hamlet **private**. This **confirms** how much she **relies** on **powerful men** — she'd rather cooperate with Claudius than her son because he offers **greater protection**.
	2) Claudius **doesn't care** that Gertrude was in **danger**, he's only **worried** that it could have been **him** — when he says "**had we been there**" (line 13) he's using the 'royal we', which means him.
	3) Claudius is **mainly concerned** about how the **scandal** will **affect him**. He wonders how he can reveal and "**excuse**" (line 32) Hamlet's crime without making the crown seem **vulnerable**.

DISHONEST	1) Gertrude **lies** to Claudius, and says that Hamlet is **mad** — she keeps it **secret** that he's only **faking madness** (unless she thinks he really is mad).
	2) Gertrude says that Hamlet "**weeps for what is done**" (line 27) to **protect** Hamlet even though he doesn't seem to **care**. She also **doesn't tell** Claudius that Hamlet **suspects him** of **killing** King Hamlet.
	3) Claudius lies to Gertrude, telling her that he's **sending Hamlet away** for his **own good**, rather than out of **fear**. He **agrees** that Hamlet is **mad**, despite his **doubts** — it's a **good excuse** to send him away. He also keeps his **plot** to **kill Hamlet secret** from her.

Act 4, Scene 2 — Hamlet Criticises Rosencrantz and Guildenstern...

- **Hamlet refuses** to tell **Rosencrantz** and **Guildenstern** anything, and **criticises** their **selfish behaviour**.

This **short scene** continues to deal with the **consequences** of Polonius's **murder**:

1) In this scene, Hamlet doesn't appear to be **sensitive** or **reflective** — he hides Polonius's body without any **concern** about his **crime**. Instead of being **shocked** by his actions, he appears **unstable** and his **faked madness** seems **real**. Hamlet's madness becomes **more ambiguous** as the play **continues**.

2) Hamlet's angry reaction to Rosencrantz and Guildenstern seems unnecessary — they're just trying to **find out** where Hamlet has **hidden** Polonius's **body**. Hamlet treats them with contempt, **offended** that they think they can **outwit** him. Hamlet's **treatment** of the **confused pair** brings some **black comedy** to an otherwise **tragic** part of the play.

3) He answers their questions in **riddles**: "**The body is with the King, but the King is not with the body**" (lines 27–28). He also **insults** them, calling Rosencrantz a "**sponge**" (line 12). Hamlet explains that Rosencrantz "**soaks up the King's countenance, his rewards, his authorities**" and warns him that Claudius will squeeze him "**dry again**" when he's finished using him. Despite Hamlet's **explanation**, Rosencrantz replies "**I understand you not**" (lines 15–22).

© PARAMOUNT / THE KOBAL COLLECTION

Act 4, Scenes 3-4

Hamlet wonders how Fortinbras can fight over a bit of irrelevant land, whilst he struggles to kill his murderous uncle.

Act 4, Scene 3 — Claudius Plans to Kill Hamlet...

- Claudius tells Hamlet that he's sending him to England with Rosencrantz and Guildenstern.
- Hamlet agrees to leave Denmark. Alone on the stage, Claudius reveals his plot to kill Hamlet.

As in the previous scene, the murder of Polonius seems to have left Hamlet frantic and unstable. Hamlet and Claudius are still trying to outsmart each other, whilst Rosencrantz and Guildenstern are confused.

1) Hamlet uses dark humour to make light of his crime, saying that Polonius is at "supper... / Not where he eats, but where 'a is eaten" (lines 17-19) — meaning that his corpse is being eaten by worms. This behaviour adds to Hamlet's apparent madness, but also shows that he's still sane enough to be witty.

2) His dislike for Claudius is barely hidden in this scene — Hamlet ridicules Claudius by describing "how a king may go a progress through the guts of a beggar" (lines 29-30). Hamlet is comparing Claudius to excrement, and unlike most of the court, he's clever enough to understand his nephew's insult.

3) Hamlet tells Claudius that he already knew of his plan to send him to England: "So is it, if thou knewest our purposes" (line 49). However, only the audience knows that Hamlet suspects Claudius of more devious motives. Claudius's actions reveal his fear of Hamlet — whether he's sane or mad, he poses a threat to the crown.

4) Claudius shows that he's still a clever politician. Instead of killing Hamlet in Denmark, he holds back, aware of Hamlet's popularity with both Gertrude and the "distracted multitude" (line 4). Claudius is constantly thinking about how to manipulate people and events to strengthen his own power and ward off any threats.

Act 4, Scene 4 — Hamlet Compares Himself with Fortinbras...

- Fortinbras enters Denmark with his army. Hamlet compares himself with Fortinbras and decides he must act.

In Act 2, Scene 2, Hamlet felt ashamed that he couldn't reach the intense emotions of the players — in this scene Hamlet feels ashamed that he's unable to act decisively like Fortinbras:

1) Hamlet describes Fortinbras as "a delicate and tender prince" (line 48) and admires his ability to act. If Fortinbras can lead innocent men to their death, Hamlet reasons that he should be able to take vengeance on Claudius when he has "cause, and will, and strength, and means" (line 45).

2) Hamlet's analysis of Fortinbras is a bit confusing. He thinks that Fortinbras's war isn't morally right, as he fights for "a little patch of ground / That hath in it no profit" (lines 18-19), yet Hamlet is still inspired by Fortinbras.

3) Hamlet decides that "from this time forth, / My thoughts be bloody" (lines 65-66). He prepares himself to finally act, yet it's interesting that Hamlet says "thoughts" rather than 'actions'. Critics have argued that, even after this moment, Hamlet's revenge only comes as a result of Claudius's actions rather than his own.

Practice Questions

Q1 Reread Act 4, Scene 1 and rewrite Gertrude's part so that it reveals more about her character.

Q2 'Apart from the ending, *Hamlet* is more of a comedy than a tragedy.' To what extent do you agree with this statement? Back up your answer with examples from the text.

Q3 Do you think that Rosencrantz and Guildenstern's actions are a betrayal of Hamlet? Refer to the text in your answer.

Q4 Using Act 4, Scene 3 as a starting point, assess who ultimately wins the battle of wits between Hamlet and Claudius.

"From this time forth, / My thoughts be bloody, or be nothing worth"

Hamlet's soliloquy in Act 4, Scene 4 was often cut from productions because the actor playing Hamlet had so many lines and the play was already so long. Luckily for us, nosy editors have dug it back up again — lucky, lucky, lucky us...

Act 4, Scenes 5-6

Scene 5 reveals the despair of Polonius's children, but Scene 6 is a bit weird — it's basically just Horatio reading a letter...

Act 4, Scene 5 — Ophelia and Laertes Both Get Mad (sort of)...

- **Ophelia** has **gone mad** from **grief** and **Gertrude** tries to **avoid seeing her**.
- **Laertes returns** with an angry mob, hungry for **revenge**, but **Claudius calms** him down.

One of the **main themes** in *Hamlet* is the **relationship** between the **state** of Denmark and the **morality** of its **ruler**. In these two scenes Denmark really is "**rotten**" — Polonius is **dead**, Ophelia is **mad** and the Danish people are **restless**.

Ophelia Goes Insane...

1) Gertrude **pities** Ophelia but **doesn't want** to see her. It's **unclear** why, but there are **several possibilities:**

   - Gertrude's **affection** for Ophelia could mean that she didn't **want** to see her in such an **awful state**.
   - She might be **feeling guilty** that **her son** has **caused** Ophelia's madness.
   - The **similarities** between the **two characters** might make Gertrude **afraid** to **see herself** in Ophelia's **madness**.

2) Whereas Hamlet may be **faking madness**, there's **no doubt** that Ophelia's **insane**. Polonius's death and Hamlet's rejection leave Ophelia alone and **without** the men that she **depended** on — she's **unable** to **function** without them.

3) Ophelia's **madness** is **shown** through her songs. They're **mostly nonsense**, but there's a **sexual undertone** that Horatio **worries** might spark **damaging rumours**. ⟸

4) These songs suggest that Ophelia has **sexuality** on her mind — perhaps the **pressures** of **remaining chaste** have led to her **madness**.

> Critics have used these songs to question Ophelia's chastity — one song is about how young men give false promises of marriage to make women sleep with them (lines 59-67).

5) Ophelia's **evident insanity symbolises** the fact that the **rotten elements** in Denmark (like **corruption** and **madness**) which were previously **hidden**, are now **becoming clearer**.

...but Laertes is Angry

> Despite their differences, Hamlet and Laertes both want to avenge their murdered fathers.

1) **Unlike** Hamlet, Laertes **immediately** seeks **revenge** for his father's **murder**, **storming** Elsinore with an **army** of **followers**. Claudius is worried about the **unrest** caused by Polonius's **death** — he's **worried** that the people are saying that "**Laertes shall be king**" (line 108).

2) However, Claudius **quickly deflects** Laertes's **rage**. Claudius realises that Laertes is **unlikely** to **calm down**, so he **encourages** him to use his rage to take his **revenge**. He **denies** any **responsibility** for Polonius's death, and says "**where th'offence is, let the great axe fall**" (line 218).

3) This scene highlights one of the **most important contrasts** of Laertes and Hamlet — whereas Claudius finds it **difficult** to **manipulate** Hamlet, he **easily uses** Laertes's **impulsive nature** to his **advantage**.

Act 4, Scene 6 — The Pirates of the North Sea...

- **Horatio** reads a **letter** from **Hamlet** which reveals that Hamlet has **foiled Claudius's plot** and is **coming back**.

1) This scene is a good **example** of a '**deus ex machina**' — Hamlet gets a **lucky rescue** from some **helpful pirates**. It also hints that **providence** is now **shaping** Hamlet's **fate**.

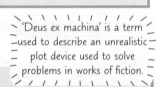

> 'Deus ex machina' is a term used to describe an unrealistic plot device used to solve problems in works of fiction.

2) It introduces **questions** about Hamlet's **morality:**

   - He **struggles** to **punish** his **guilty** uncle, but thinks **nothing** of sending his **old friends**, Rosencrantz and Guildenstern, to their **deaths**.
   - Hamlet also rewards the **pirates** who **attacked** his ship: "**I am to do a good turn for them**" (line 21). Hamlet seems to be making **questionable moral decisions** that echo **Claudius**, and even writes "**I have words to speak in thine ear will make thee dumb**" (lines 23-24) echoing the events of King Hamlet's **murder**.

3) In contrast to Hamlet's **previous thoughts** about **death**, this letter shows that he now **wants to live** — it's **written** with an **energy** that makes him seem **positive** about **life** and it uses phrases like "**wouldst fly death**" (line 23). This makes Hamlet's **death** in Act 5, Scene 2 even more **tragic**, as the next scene reveals Claudius's **plot** to **kill** the prince.

Act 4, Scene 7

Claudius thinks that Hamlet has been safely taken to his death, but then a mysterious letter arrives...

Hamlet's Back, but Claudius has a Plan...

- **Claudius** finds out that **Hamlet** isn't **dead**, and **persuades Laertes** to kill Hamlet in a **fencing match** using a **sharpened**, **poisoned sword**. Claudius also suggests that they **poison** the **wine** in case Hamlet **wins**.
- **Gertrude** reveals that **Ophelia** has **drowned** in what seem like **suspicious circumstances**.

This scene **confirms** Claudius's **role** as the **villain** of the play. It also creates **sympathy** for Hamlet, who Claudius describes as "**Most generous, and free from all contriving**" (line 134) **in spite** of the prince's **crimes**.

Claudius Keeps on Plotting to Kill Hamlet

1) Claudius continues to use **deception** — instead of allowing Laertes to take revenge **directly**, he'd rather use **trickery**. Ironically, the **devious scheming** which helped him to **seize** the crown will ultimately lead to his death.

2) Claudius feels that he **can't kill** Hamlet **himself** because the prince is **popular** with the **Danish people** and **Gertrude** — he doesn't want to **lose** his **wife** or **kingdom**. Thinking quickly, Claudius works out a way to solve the problem — a **duel satisfies** Laertes and **gets rid of** Hamlet.

© CASTLE ROCK ENTERTAINMENT / THE KOBAL COLLECTION / MOUNTAIN, PETER

3) Claudius continues to **manipulate** Laertes — he uses flattery to **persuade** him to **agree** to his plan: "**they say you shine**" (line 72). Claudius argues that his **revenge** will show Laertes's **love** for his **father**. This **mirrors** the Ghost's conversation with Hamlet: "**If thou didst ever thy dear father love**" (1.5.23).

4) This scene proves that **corruption** is **increasing** in Claudius's court — Claudius and Laertes decide on **three separate deceptions** to ensure Hamlet's **death** (a sharpened sword, a poisoned blade and poisoned wine).

5) **Unlike** Hamlet, Laertes will **stop at nothing** to get his revenge and would even "**cut his throat i'th'church**" (line 125) — the very **same act** that Hamlet **refused** to do to Claudius in **Act 3, Scene 3**. Claudius's **response** also shows how **spiritually different** Claudius and Hamlet are — Claudius agrees with Laertes that "**Revenge should have no bounds**" (line 127) because he **isn't concerned** with the **fate** of Hamlet's **soul**.

Ophelia Drowns but it's a Suspicious Death

Ophelia is associated with flowers throughout the play — this highlights her fragile, innocent nature.

1) Gertrude's **description** of Ophelia's **death** is **out of place** with the rest of the scene — the imagery used is **lyrical**, **beautiful** and almost **mythical**. Gertrude's **strange account** raises a lot of **questions**:

- It's **unclear** why the person **watching** Ophelia's death didn't **help** her (see p.33).
- It might have been **suicide** — Ophelia **didn't resist**, despite floating for "**awhile**" (line 176).
- Gertrude's description seems **detached**: "**There is a willow grows askant the brook**" (line 166). It doesn't sound like an **emotional description** of a **traumatic** event.

2) As soon as Laertes leaves, Claudius tells Gertrude "**How much I had to do to calm his rage!**" (line 192) but Claudius **hasn't discouraged** Laertes's **anger**, he's just **used** it for his **own ends**. Ophelia's tragic death occurs **between** a **murderous plot** and Claudius's **lie**, which **emphasises** that she's an **innocent victim** of a **corrupt world**.

Practice Questions

Q1 'In Act 4, Scenes 5 and 7 we see Claudius at his most devious and brilliant.'
To what extent do you agree with this statement? Back up your answer with examples from the text.

Q2 Reread Hamlet's letter in Act 4, Scene 6 and write a first-hand account of the events from his perspective.

"To show yourself in deed your father's son"

It might just be me, but it seems a bit like Shakespeare made up Act 4, Scene 6 on the spot... 'So Hamlet's on his way to be killed, yeah? But then suddenly there are these... er... Ninjas? Pirates? And they're all like — Hey come join us! And Hamlet goes oh all right.'

Act 5, Scene 1

In the cemetery, a gravedigger digs a grave (funnily enough) and brings some wisdom and dark humour to the play...

Hamlet and Laertes *Fight* at *Ophelia's Funeral*...

- The **Gravedigger** talks to a **second man** as he digs a **grave** while **Hamlet** and **Horatio watch**.
- Hamlet finds the **skull** of **Yorick**, the old court **jester**, and **discusses death** with Horatio.
- The **funeral procession** arrives and Hamlet finds out that **Ophelia's dead**. The **priest** suggests that she might have committed **suicide** and **questions** whether she should have a **Christian burial**.
- **Laertes grieves** for Ophelia, and Hamlet **fights** with him over who **loved** her the **most**.

This scene is **important** for the **development** of Hamlet's character:

1) This scene could be **symbolic** of Hamlet's **own funeral** as Hamlet comes to **terms** with the **inevitability** of his **death**.
2) By **revealing himself** to Laertes, Hamlet sets off a **chain of events** that leads to his **duel** with Laertes and his **subsequent death**.

Some Christians believed that if you didn't resist death, this still counted as suicide.

Ophelia *May Have Committed Suicide*

1) Laertes is **angry** that Ophelia's funeral has "**maimèd rites**" (line 215) because the **church** thinks it was **suicide**. Laertes feels that his sister's **funeral** reflects badly on him and claims that Ophelia will be "**a ministering angel**" while the priest will "**liest howling**" for dishonouring his family (lines 237-238).
2) This scene **emphasises** Ophelia's **virginity** — for example, Laertes describes his sister's "**fair and unpolluted flesh**" (line 235). This **creates pathos** and makes her death more **tragic** — if Ophelia was chaste and therefore not **promiscuous** then Hamlet's **rejection** was misguided.
3) Hamlet claims that he'd **eat a crocodile** out of love for Ophelia to **highlight** how **strong** his **feelings** for her are (line 272). However, this image is **absurd** and Hamlet could be **reacting angrily** to Laertes's attempts to make his **love** seem **superior**.
4) It's strange that Hamlet never seems to **feel guilty** for Ophelia's death — the only time he almost takes **responsibility** is when he blames Polonius's death on his **madness** in **Act 5, Scene 2**. Some **critics** have argued that if Hamlet had taken **full responsibility** for his **crimes**, he wouldn't have been able to **bear** the **psychological trauma**.

Hamlet *and* Laertes *Don't Get On*

1) In this scene, Laertes and Hamlet **finally meet**. It's as if Shakespeare keeps them **apart** until the end of the play.
2) Hamlet seems to have **mixed feelings** about Laertes — he **initially** calls him a "**very noble youth**" when he sees him (line 220), but then **attacks him**, saying "**I will fight with him upon this theme / Until my eyelids will no longer wag**" (lines 262-263).
3) Hamlet **praises** Laertes for being "**noble**" because he **recognises** that Laertes **actively defends** his family's **honour**. Hamlet wishes that he was **more like him**.
4) Hamlet attacks Laertes because he thinks Laertes's **love** and **grief** for Ophelia are **shallow** — Laertes uses **hyperbole** and **numbers** to make his grief seem more **impressive**, when it actually makes it seem **silly** and **inappropriate**.
5) Their **fight** is also **fuelled** by the fact that they're like **love rivals** fighting over who **loved** Ophelia the **most**. When Laertes leaps into the grave to hold Ophelia, there's an **incestuous undertone** (see p.36) and Hamlet questions whether Laertes is just trying "**To outface [him] with leaping in her grave**" (line 274).

© PARAMOUNT / THE KOBAL COLLECTION

Act 5, Scene 1

The Gravedigger has Two Important Roles

The Gravedigger and his companion are called "clowns" in the stage directions, but the word 'clown' meant peasant, and didn't necessarily mean that they were funny.

1) The Gravedigger has **several functions**:

- His **conversation** about Ophelia's **suspicious death** reinforces the **ambiguous nature** of the play.
- He represents the **common classes** and is an 'everyman' figure. This shows that Hamlet is a **man of the people**, because he **shares** their **concerns** and **talks** to them almost as if they're **equals**.
- He seems to **know** a lot about the **beginning** and the **end of time** (lines 30-60). This **timelessness emphasises** that his **messages** about death apply to **everyone**.

2) The Gravedigger's **two main roles** are to **provide comedy** and to **challenge Hamlet's views**:

COMEDY

- The Gravedigger provides some of the most **obvious comedy** in *Hamlet* — his **jokes** are **clear** and designed to **amuse** the **commoners** in the pit of the Globe Theatre. For example the Gravedigger claims that it **doesn't matter** if Hamlet is **cured** of his **madness** in **England** as "**There the men are as mad as he**" (lines 152-153).
- The **comedy** comes partly from the fact that the Gravedigger is outsmarting Hamlet, a person of a higher **social class** — this happens **frequently** in **Shakespeare's plays** e.g. Feste in *Twelfth Night*.
- The Gravedigger uses a **morbid tone** but he interprets **death** in a **darkly humorous** way. This **contrasts** with the **serious mood** of Hamlet's "**To be, or not to be**" soliloquy in **Act 3, Scene 1**.

CHALLENGE

- The Gravedigger's **carefree attitude** forces Hamlet to **reevaluate** his ideas about **death**. The Gravedigger is **making fun** of Hamlet when he claims that the **grave** he's digging is **his own**, but he's making an **important general point** — in **death**, **rank** and **material possessions** don't **matter**.
- The Gravedigger doesn't seem to **respect social class** — he **complains** that Ophelia is only allowed a **Christian burial** because her family is **powerful**. Hamlet **realises** that **everyone is equal** in death when he sees that the Gravedigger treats all skulls **the same**. Everyone is **forgotten** in the end.

Hamlet Starts to Think about Death Differently

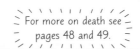

For more on death see pages 48 and 49.

1) **Throughout** the play, Hamlet **fixates** on the **spiritual consequences** of **suicide** and **murder**, but in this scene he's just as **interested** in the **physical** side of **death**. Hamlet **imagines** how the flesh has **rotted** from the **skulls** (lines 75 and 185), and **realises** that everyone becomes "**dust**", even men like **Alexander the Great** (lines 199-201).

2) This is **important** because it makes Hamlet **question** the **importance** of his **dead father**. In Act 5, King Hamlet is **barely mentioned**, and Hamlet starts to use **personal pronouns** such as "**I**", "**mine**" and "**my**" more **often**. This shows that he's taking **ownership** of his **quest** for **revenge**, instead of **feeling** like it's been **forced** upon him.

3) Hamlet's examination of **Yorick's skull** is important because it forces Hamlet to see his own **inevitable fate**. Like Yorick, Hamlet has become the **court jester** in some ways — he's **constantly** making **jokes** throughout the play. It could be argued that this **shared role** makes Hamlet **realise** that he will also **share** Yorick's **fate**.

4) The fact that Yorick's skull makes Hamlet think of his **childhood** also **symbolises** the fact that he's **lost his innocence**. Hamlet is fully aware of what **awaits him** in the **next scene** and knows that he has a **responsibility** to take **action**.

Practice Questions

Q1 'Act 5, Scene 1 is the most important scene in the play for the development of Hamlet's character.' To what extent do you agree with this statement? Back up your answer with examples from the text.

Q2 Assess whether Hamlet's actions at Ophelia's funeral were more caused by his love for her, or by his anger at Laertes. Do you think that Hamlet felt at all responsible for Ophelia's death? Back up your answer with evidence from the text.

"Hold off the earth awhile, / Till I have caught her once more"

According to the Gravedigger, Hamlet's 30 years old — this may not seem like a big deal, but it confuses a lot of critics, who think that his odd behaviour throughout the play can be explained by the fact that he's a teenager. Talk about stereotyping...

Act 5, Scene 2

The final scene of the play centres on Hamlet's duel with Laertes, and it's very much a case of last man standing...

Everyone Dies, but Fortinbras Wins...

- **Hamlet tells Horatio** how he **switched letters** on the ship and sent **Rosencrantz** and **Guildenstern** to their **deaths**.
- **Osric**, a **foolish courtier**, tells Hamlet that **Claudius** wants him to fence with **Laertes**. Hamlet **agrees**, despite Horatio's **warnings**. Although Hamlet **apologises**, Laertes still wants **revenge**.
- The two men **fight** and Hamlet is **stabbed** by the **poisoned sword**. After more fighting, the two blades are **accidentally swapped** and Laertes is **also stabbed** by the **poisoned blade**.
- **Gertrude toasts** Hamlet and **drinks the poisoned wine**. Laertes **reveals** that Claudius is **responsible**.
- Hamlet **stabs the king** with the **poisoned sword**, then **forces him** to **drink his poisoned wine**. Claudius and Laertes **die**. As Hamlet dies, he tells Horatio to **explain** what **happened** and that **Fortinbras** should be the **next king**.
- Fortinbras **arrives** and is **shocked** by the **tragic scene**. He agrees to **hear** Horatio's **story** and makes sure that Hamlet is given a **soldier's funeral**. Fortinbras will become **King of Denmark**.

In the final scene, the **anticipated violence takes place**.

1) The **duel symbolises** the battle between **goodness** and **corruption** — Hamlet's fighting for **morality** and his father's **honour** and Laertes is fighting on behalf of **Claudius** and his **dishonest** court. It's the dramatic climax of the play.

2) There are a lot of **dramatic concerns** in this scene. The fight only lasts a **few lines** so the director needs to decide **how long** the characters should fight **on stage**, in an **already long play**. Shakespeare's play also **doesn't explain** how the blades are **swapped**.

© CASTLE ROCK ENTERTAINMENT / THE KOBAL COLLECTION / MOUNTAIN, PETER

Hamlet has a Changed View of the World

In this scene Hamlet **takes control** of his **own actions**. He **decides**:

> Hamlet seems to believe in (Protestant) Calvinist predestination — all events happen by God's will.

- **that he'll stop hesitating**. He doesn't **regret** the **impulsive** action that **killed** Rosencrantz and Guildenstern. He intends to **act** again to get his revenge and says **"praised be rashness"** (line 7).
- **to give in to fate**. Hamlet decides that **"There's a divinity that shapes our ends"** (line 10). Rosencrantz and Guildenstern's deaths **"are not near [his] conscience"** as that was their **fate** (line 58). Some critics argue that this **betrays** Hamlet's **principles** up to this point, but others argue that Hamlet just **wants to believe** that there's a **reason** behind **what happens**, even if man can't know it.
- **that he'll be damned** if he **doesn't kill** Claudius. This is the **opposite** of what he **thought before**. He now believes that Claudius's **sins** mean that he can seek **revenge** in **"perfect conscience"** (line 67).
- **to take ownership** of his quest for **honour** and **revenge**. He starts using **possessive pronouns** like **"He that hath killed *my* King and whored *my* mother"** (line 64) to show that the Ghost **doesn't control him**.
- **to start considering others**. Before, Hamlet was **only concerned** with his **own quest** but now he wants **forgiveness** from Laertes (lines 75-78). It seems **strange** that Hamlet **blames** Polonius's **murder** on his **madness** when he claims that he's **faking it** throughout the play. Perhaps Hamlet **accepts** that he's **passed very close** to **genuine madness**.

Hamlet still Hates the Abuse of Language

1) Hamlet **dislikes characters** that **abuse language** — he mocks Polonius's **ramblings** and Laertes's use of **hyperbole**.

2) It's therefore not surprising that Osric, who's fond of **pompous** and **complicated** speech, is an **easy target** for Hamlet. Hamlet **parodies** him by giving long-winded answers: **"his definement suffers no perdition in you, though, I know, to divide him inventorially would dizzy th'arithmetic of memory"** (lines 112 -114).

3) By making **unlikable characters** abuse language, Shakespeare shows that **words** can be **misleading** and **dangerous**.

Act 5, Scene 2

There's *Justice* in the *Play's Conclusion* but not for *Every Character*

1) The **themes** of **revenge** and **justice** come together when Hamlet **kills Claudius** — even though he only acts once he finds himself in **extreme circumstances** .

2) By the end of the play, Claudius is **isolated**. He's the **single villain** and all his **potential co-conspirators** (Polonius, Rosencrantz, Guildenstern, Laertes and Gertrude) are **dead**.

3) It's clear that Claudius **deserves** his **fate**, but it's more **ambiguous** whether everyone else gets what they **deserve**:

GERTRUDE

1) Gertrude's fate seems **undeserved** — the majority of the play suggests that she was **innocent**, or at least **naïve** of most of the **crimes** that Hamlet **accused** her of **committing**.

2) She might have **known** that the wine was **poisoned** and drank it to **save** her son. Even if she didn't know, she takes Hamlet's **side** and **ignores** Claudius's **command** not to drink it.

ROSENCRANTZ & GUILDENSTERN

1) Rosencrantz and Guildenstern's deaths are **announced** in this scene — their deaths raise questions about Hamlet's **morals**. They did **betray** Hamlet, but death seems like a **harsh** punishment — Hamlet doesn't even **allow** them to **confess** their **sins** before death: "**Not shriving time allowed**" (line 47). This contrasts with Hamlet's attitude to Claudius's sins in **Act 3, Scene 3**.

2) Even Horatio seems **surprised** that Hamlet shrugs off his two friends' **deaths** as a **necessary evil** in a battle between "**mighty opposites**" (line 62).

LAERTES

1) Laertes, in the **role** of **traditional revenge hero**, gets **justice** by **killing Hamlet** but he also **dies**. This raises questions of whether Laertes's death was **deserved** — he was only trying to **avenge** his father.

2) Laertes's death is the **result** of his **rash** decision to become part of Claudius's **plan** to kill Hamlet. He **makes sure** that he chooses the **poisoned blade** even after he's **accepted** Hamlet's offer of **love**. His **honour** is also called into **question** when he scratches Hamlet during a **break** in the fight.

3) Because Laertes **accepts** that he's "**justly killed with [his] own treachery**" (line 301), the **audience** accepts it too. He also **realises** that his **vengeance** isn't **honourable**: "**it is almost against my conscience**" (line 290).

HAMLET

1) Hamlet's death can be seen as **deserved** — though Hamlet never takes **full responsibility** for Polonius's **murder**, it's fair that Laertes **kills him** for his **crime**.

2) Hamlet is **justly punished** for Polonius's murder. However, Laertes **forgives** Hamlet in his **dying moments**, saying that Hamlet isn't any more **responsible** for the situation than Laertes is (lines 324-325). This suggests that Hamlet's death **wasn't justified**.

FORTINBRAS

1) Fortinbras becomes **King of Denmark** — he's not the **perfect man** but he **survives** and **regains** his **lost lands** because he has the **ability** to **think** *and* **act**. Both Laertes and Hamlet **fail** because they can only **think** or **act**.

2) Fortinbras's **capabilities** mean that he's the **best candidate** for the **throne**. In **contrast** to the **corrupt court** dead on the floor, he's a **strong leader**.

3) Fortinbras is a **shrewd politician** who seems to have the **best parts** of **Claudius** and **King Hamlet** in his **character**. He orders that Hamlet has a **soldier's burial** — Fortinbras could be **aware** of Hamlet's **popularity**, since a soldier's funeral for Hamlet seems **ironic**, and knows that this would **please** the Danish people.

Practice Questions

Q1 'All of the deaths in *Hamlet* are the direct result of each character's individual flaws — they all cause their own downfall.' To what extent do you agree with this statement? Back up your answer with examples from the text.

Q2 Do you think that Hamlet would ever have acted if circumstances had not forced him to do so? Back up your answer with examples from the text.

"Treachery! Seek it out. / It is here, Hamlet. Hamlet, thou art slain"

After an incredibly long haul, we've finally reached the end of the play. Never fear, there's plenty more of this text guide still to come. It's the end, it's the end, yippee, yes, hooray. 'Play' — 'hooray'. That almost rhymed... I'm a poet and I didn't even have awareness of it.

Hamlet

Wherever Hamlet goes, questions follow after — we don't know what he's thinking, why he delays, whether he's mad...
I used to worry that I was mad until Doctor Cootväller told me I was just paranoid. He's not a bad Psychiatrist for an aardvark.

Hamlet's an *Introspective Deep Thinker*

If you're introspective, you tend to spend a lot of time assessing your own thoughts and feelings.

It's **difficult** for the **audience** to **understand** Hamlet when there's **more** to him than **meets the eye**:

1) Hamlet never **reveals** his **true thoughts** about the **murderous task** he's been given — even in his conversations with Horatio he remains **secretive**.

2) His language is full of **double meanings** and **riddles**, e.g. **"The body is with the King, but the King is not with the body."** (4.2.27-28). This makes it hard to work out what he **really thinks**.

3) This is frustrating because Hamlet is not a man of **action** — we can only **learn** about him through what he chooses to **say**.

4) Hamlet is **obsessed** with questions that can't be **answered** — he constantly **doubts** and **challenges** the **world** around him. His thoughtful nature plays a major role in **delaying** his revenge.

© Geraint Lewis/Rex Features

He's a *Very Moral* Character

1) Hamlet has a very clear sense of **'right'** and **'wrong'** and believes that other people **share** his moral views. Claudius and Gertrude's **actions shatter** his **moral faith** and lead to his melancholic **"transformation"** (2.2.5).

2) He doesn't care about **material things** like the **crown** — he's more concerned with issues of **morality** like his father's **murder** and his mother's **"o'erhasty marriage"** (2.2.57). The Ghost's **revelations** force him to question the **morality** of the **world** — with all sense of **righteousness** and **justice removed**, he starts to think about the idea of **suicide**.

Hamlet's morality prevents him from committing suicide. He fears that he would go to Hell if he took his own life (see p.49).

3) Hamlet spends the play trying to **overcome** his **doubts** and regain his **faith** in **goodness**. He's **reluctant** to seek revenge because of the **moral** and **spiritual issues** involved in committing **murder**. Despite his **hatred** of Claudius, the Ghost has to **force** him to act.

4) He can only justify murdering Claudius by deciding that mankind has no control over their **destiny**: **"There's a divinity that shapes our ends"** (5.2.10). Hamlet may take comfort in the idea of fate, because it means he's not **responsible** for the murder of Claudius.

Hamlet *Delays* his *Revenge* on Claudius

There are many **reasons** why Hamlet **might have** struggled to kill Claudius:

1) Hamlet's **introspective nature** means that he must **think** everything through **before acting**.

2) Hamlet's **Christian morals** clash with his **duty** as a **revenger** (see p.42). The Christian view is that only **God** has the right to take **vengeance** — Hamlet must **overcome** this belief before he can take revenge.

3) There's **uncertainty** over the Ghost's **revelations** and whether or not they can be **trusted** (see p.40 and p.41).

4) Some critics have argued that Hamlet's task is a **patriotic duty** — he must save his country from **Fortinbras's invasion** as well as **internal corruption**. Hamlet could have acted **sooner** and made his dispute **public** (by raising an army like Laertes did) but he **avoids** anything that might make Denmark appear **vulnerable**.

5) Shakespeare was writing at a time of political, social and religious **uncertainty**. *Hamlet* could just be **echoing** these widespread feelings of insecurity — the play is full of **contradictions, inconsistencies** and **uncertainties**. The reasons for Hamlet's delay might be supposed to **remain uncertain**.

6) **Freud** argues that Hamlet has an **Oedipus complex** (see p.66) — Claudius has done what Hamlet **wants to do** as he's **killed** King Hamlet and **slept** with Gertrude. Hamlet can't kill Claudius because it would be like **killing himself**. **Revenge** would be like **suicide**, which explains Hamlet's **confusion** about the two issues.

7) Critics such as **Voltaire** and **T.S. Eliot** argue that *Hamlet's* just **badly written** — the delay can't be **explained** because Shakespeare didn't write Hamlet's character well enough to make any **sense** of his behaviour.

Hamlet

There are Questions over Hamlet's Madness

See p.44 and p.45 for more on madness.

Most critics believe that Hamlet was only **pretending** to be mad:

1) Hamlet himself says "**I essentially am not in madness, / But mad in craft**" (3.4.188-189) — this suggests that he **feigns** madness to convince Claudius that he's not a **threat** so he can collect **evidence** against his uncle.

2) Hamlet only **appears insane** in front of people he **suspects** will **report** back to Claudius — in front of **everyone else**, Hamlet acts **sane**. **Only Claudius** and his **followers** think Hamlet is mad (but even they have **doubts**).

3) Shakespeare tends to use **genuine madness** for **dramatic value** — for example, he uses Lady Macbeth's madness to emphasise her overwhelming **guilt** and build up to her **suicide**. Hamlet's madness doesn't have this **purpose**.

Some critics believe that Hamlet was **genuinely insane**, or that he **goes insane** because of the **strain** of feigning madness:

1) The **original sources** of the story **clearly state** that Hamlet's character only **feigns madness**. Shakespeare **deliberately** introduces **doubt** — Hamlet's **reasoned thought** is **undermined** by acts of **impulsiveness**.

2) Hamlet shows some **symptoms** of a disturbed mental state:

- He constantly **loses** his train of thought and doesn't reach any **conclusions**.
- He has **sleepless** nights filled with **nightmares**.
- He's **obsessed** with **secrecy**.
- He believes a **Ghost** drives him to murder (see p.41).
- He **distances** himself from the people he **loves**.

Ultimately Shakespeare makes Hamlet's mental state **ambiguous** so that it's up to the **audience** to **decide** if he's sane or not.

Hamlet's Use of Humour suggests he's Sane

1) **Critics** have argued that Hamlet's **humour** proves his **sanity**. Hamlet **stays sane** by finding dark humour in his **situation**: "**Thrift, thrift, Horatio. The funeral baked meats / Did coldly furnish forth the marriage tables**" (1.2.180-181).

2) Hamlet never misses an **opportunity** to **mock** the other characters — he uses humour to **insult** Polonius, Rosencrantz and Guildenstern (see p.35 and p.39), and to **make fun** of other people's **stupidity**. For example, he tricks Osric into first agreeing that "**It is indifferent cold**" and then that "**It is very sultry**" (5.2.97-100).

3) Hamlet's **humour** is always **appropriate** to the **situation** — it's possible that a **madman** wouldn't have this **awareness**.

He has a Complicated Relationship with Women

1) Hamlet believes that his mother's marriage to his uncle is a sign of her **immorality**. His anger at Gertrude isn't simply because of her **betrayal** — it's also because of her sexual "**appetite**". Hamlet is even **disgusted** by the **memory** of how she acted with his **father**: "**she would hang on him**" (1.2.143-144).

2) Hamlet despairs with his **mother's behaviour** — **marrying Claudius** so soon after King Hamlet's **death**. He then **transfers** his **feelings** towards **Gertrude** to **all women**. He calls them '**frail**' and **morally weak** because of what he sees as their **promiscuity**.

3) His love for Ophelia seems **genuine**, but he acts strangely in front of her, suggesting he's **using her** to maintain his **mask of madness**. It's difficult to **justify** his **behaviour** towards her — if Hamlet isn't mad then he knowingly treats her cruelly. He also **denies** loving her, "**I loved you not**" (3.1.119), until after her **death**, when she's **free** from **earthly desires**.

Practice Questions

Q1 Imagine you are a psychiatrist who is deciding if Hamlet is insane. Write a report detailing your findings.

Q2 'It is both the pivot about which the play turns and its downfall.' To what extent do you agree with this criticism of Hamlet's delayed revenge? Back up your answer with examples from the text.

"You would pluck out the heart of my mystery"

So many questions and we're only just getting started on these pesky characters... The important thing to remember is that whatever your opinion on the characters, you must support it with evidence from the text. It's all about arguing convincingly.

Claudius

Claudius is Hamlet's ~~slightly~~ very unpleasant uncle. Motivated purely by selfish desires, his deviousness knows no bounds. He represents the worst in human nature — lust, greed and corruption, but he's actually not a bad king...

He's the **Main Antagonist** in the play

An antagonist is a character who provides opposition to the protagonist (in this case Hamlet).

1) Claudius **killed** his brother. He's one of the main causes of Hamlet's **anger**, **confusion** and apparent **madness**.

2) Although it's clear that Claudius is a **murderous villain**, he's not completely **evil**. He's **morally weak**, and will do anything to seize and hang onto power, but he's not **unfeeling**:

© Alastair Muir/Rex Features

- He's **genuinely sorry** for Polonius's death — **"O, heavy deed!"** (4.1.12).
- He seems to **love** Gertrude — he resolves to kill Hamlet, but **refuses** to do so with his own hand for Gertrude's sake.
- He treats Ophelia with **kindness**, even though he **uses her** as part of his plans to deceive Hamlet: **"Give her good watch, I pray you"** (4.5.75).

His **Selfishness Defines** him

The other men are concerned with justice, revenge and morality.

1) Claudius is only interested in maintaining **power**. This **selfish** behaviour **contrasts** with the other characters.

2) As the play progresses, Claudius's increasing **paranoia** makes him even more **concerned** with his own position. His **ambitions always** come before those he cares about:

- When Gertrude tells him that Hamlet has killed Polonius, Claudius is **unconcerned** that Gertrude might have been in danger — he's only worried about his **own safety**.
- He's also **thinking** about himself when he **consoles** Laertes after Polonius's death. He **manipulates** Laertes's grief for his **own end**, by using Laertes as a way of killing Hamlet: **"What would you undertake / To show yourself in deed your father's son"** (4.7.123-124) .
- He could stop Gertrude drinking the poison, but he doesn't because it will **implicate** him in the plot.

Claudius is an **Immoral Character**

1) Claudius seizes the Danish throne whilst Hamlet, the natural heir, is **absent**. Even though this wasn't **illegal** in Denmark, this plot would have seemed **Machiavellian** to an English audience used to a **hereditary monarchy**.

> **Machiavellian Politics**
>
> Niccolò **Machiavelli** (1469 – 1527) developed a new way of **political thinking** — he argued that rulers were **justified** in using **immoral** and **unjust** behaviour to keep control, e.g. brute force, deceit and threats. Whether Shakespeare actually read Machiavelli is unclear, but he was certainly **aware** of these ideas.

2) Religion was an **important** part of most people's lives in the seventeenth century. Claudius holds **traditional religious beliefs**, but he ignores them in order to secure his position:

- By killing King Hamlet, Claudius goes **against** the **will of God**. Most European countries believed in **divine right**, which meant that the king's powers were given by God, so kings were only **answerable** to God.
- **Biblical comparisons** highlight the **seriousness** of Claudius's crime. He compares himself to **Cain**, calling his crime **"the primal eldest curse"** (3.3.37) and the Ghost calls him a **"serpent"** (1.5.39), linking him to **Satan**.

3) Claudius's love for Gertrude seems **sincere**, but his marriage to her is also **selfish** — it helps his claim to the throne. Their marriage shows Claudius's **disregard** for religious law as it would have been seen as not only **illegal** but **immoral** in Elizabethan times — the Bible **forbade** women from marrying their husband's brother.

Claudius

He's a *Clever* and *Talented Leader*

1) For all Claudius's **flaws**, he's a pretty **talented** ruler and he knows all about **politics**.

2) His **intelligence** and **capabilities** are clear from his **first speech** in Act 1, Scene 2. He **inspires** his court and country, speaks about his **brother's death** and deals with the **potential conflict** with Norway:

- Claudius is afraid of **rebellion**. He juxtaposes the king's death with an image of himself as a caring ruler to create a sense of **national solidarity**: "**our whole kingdom / To be contracted in one brow of woe**" (1.2.3-4).
- Claudius takes on the role of **chief mourner** and the Danish people **unite** behind him in their suffering.
- He takes **decisive** action to **resolve** the situation in Norway by sending two of his ambassadors there.

Claudius is an opportunist — he uses Polonius's murder and Laertes's grief as part of his plot against Hamlet.

He *Manipulates People* with *Language*

1) King Hamlet was a **great** and **brave warrior**, but Claudius is **sly**, **cunning** and **underhand** — even his rise to power was **devious** and **cowardly**, killing his brother by pouring poison in his ear.

2) Claudius can **manipulate** other people through his clever use of **language** — he controls people "**With witchcraft of his wit**"(1.5.43). The **poison** he pours in King Hamlet's ear **symbolises** his ability to wound using poisonous words and lies.

3) He frequently **varies** his use of language to enhance his power:

- He addresses the court in the **second person**, using "you", "us" and "our", e.g. "**our dear brother's death**" (1.2.1) He switches between using the **royal** 'we' to assert his power, and addressing the crowd **personally** to get them on side.
- He uses his language to **suppress people** — his treatment of Laertes in their conversations together is a good example of this. He repeatedly **questions** him, without waiting for a reply "**was your father dear to you? / Or are you like the painting of a sorrow, / A face without a heart?**" (4.7.106-108).
- When he talks to Hamlet, in public and in private, he uses **complimentary** language: "'**Tis sweet and commendable in your nature, Hamlet**" (1.2.87). This makes Hamlet's objections to him seem **petty**, as the public only sees Claudius's apparent **love** for his nephew and Hamlet's angry reaction to him.

His *Cunning* and *Deviousness* are his own *Downfall*

1) Claudius is ultimately **too clever** for his own good. He's not convinced that his plan to use a **sharpened sword** and a **poisoned blade** will kill Hamlet, so Claudius also introduces a third fail-safe — the **poisoned goblet** which kills him.

2) When Hamlet sees his **mother die** at Claudius's hands, he's **finally able** to bring himself to kill his uncle. Claudius's plot **backfires horribly** — he becomes a **victim** of his own **cunning** and **cowardice**. **Ironically**, it's his **own devious tactics** that cause his **downfall**, and not a **planned revenge plot** by Hamlet.

3) This gives the audience a sense of **justice** — the villain is punished and order is **restored** under Fortinbras.

Practice Questions

Q1 'Claudius was a bad brother, but a good king.' How far do you agree with this statement? Back up your answer with examples from the text.

Q2 Reread Act 3, Scene 2, lines 145-279, and rewrite the events from Claudius's point of view. Think about the way in which Shakespeare presents his character in order to work out how he would have been feeling.

Q3 If Hamlet had never found out that Claudius killed his father, do you think that Claudius would have succeeded in getting Hamlet on his side? Back up your answer with examples from the text.

"O villain, villain, smiling, damnèd villain!"

No, Hamlet's not talking about Batman's arch-nemesis, he's actually talking about Claudius. As you can tell, he was not best pleased to find out that his uncle had killed his father. Everyone knows that Claudius is the villain of the piece — even Claudius himself...

Gertrude

Hamlet's an okay guy — just don't make any 'mum' jokes at his expense... He doesn't take them very well.
This analysis of Gertrude's character should go some way to explaining why he has such a sense of humour failure...

Gertrude is an **Ambiguous Character**

© PARAMOUNT / THE KOBAL COLLECTION

1) There's a lot that Shakespeare **doesn't** tell us about Gertrude. She doesn't have any **soliloquies** to **reveal** how she feels and she speaks in quite a **reserved** way.

2) She comes across as **graceful** and **charming**. However, you could argue that these qualities are **superficial**, and she just uses them to attract powerful men.

3) As Queen she holds a position of **power** and **authority**, but at times she comes across as too **trusting** and **naive**. For example, she drinks the poisoned wine despite Claudius's warning, and seems genuinely **shocked** that it's poisoned: "**No, no, the drink, the drink!**" (5.2.303).

4) Shakespeare leaves certain **aspects** of Gertrude's character **ambiguous**:

   - It's unclear if her marriage to Claudius is out of **love** or the desire to protect her own **power** and **status**.
   - It's unclear whether she **believes** Hamlet's claim that he is "**not in madness**" (3.4.188), or whether she **claims** to believe him in order to **calm** him down and **protect** herself.
   - There are **hints** that Hamlet **suspected** that she committed **adultery** before King Hamlet's death.

Gertrude cares about **Appearance**

1) Gertrude comes across well in **social situations**, where her **grace** and **charm** are obvious. For example, when she asks Rosencrantz and Guildenstern to spend time with Hamlet, she **flatters** them and phrases it as a **favour** to her, rather than an order: "**If it will please you / To show us so much gentry and good will**" (2.2.21-22). As Queen she's used to being obeyed, but she knows how to use **language** to make people **want** to obey her.

2) Gertrude's **shallow nature** is emphasised by the fact that she seems to care more about **appearances** than **reality**. For example, she tells Hamlet to "**cast thy nighted colour off**" (1.2.68) — she wants Hamlet to **stop grieving**, but she explains herself by telling him to give up the **appearance** of **mourning**.

3) This can make her seem **fake** and **superficial**. For example, in **private** she says that she "**will not speak**" (4.5.1) with Ophelia, but at Ophelia's **public funeral** she speaks kindly of her: "**Sweets to the sweet!**" (5.1.239). She also **romanticises** Ophelia's death to make it sound **beautiful** rather than tragic: "**There is a willow grows askant the brook**" (4.7.166). She **focuses** on the way the scene **looked** instead of what happened.

She **Relies** on **Men** to maintain her **Position**

1) Gertrude's **selfish desires** mean that she's concerned with **self-preservation**, just like Claudius is. She **relies** heavily on men in order to keep her life of **comfort** and her position of **authority**.

2) She dislikes **confrontation**, and **avoids** it wherever possible. She tries to keep the **peace** between Claudius and Hamlet, but this means that her **loyalties are often divided** — when Hamlet tells her that Claudius is a "**murderer and a villain**" (3.4.97) she says "**thou hast cleft my heart in twain**" (3.4.157).

In Act 3, Scene 4, Gertrude speaks very **little** and seems to **believe** what Hamlet says. She also asks for his **guidance**: "**What shall I do?**" (3.4.181) .	However, after her **confrontation** with Hamlet, she goes to **Claudius** and tells him that Hamlet has killed Polonius. It shows that she's also **loyal** to her husband.

3) Gertrude could be attracted to Claudius, a **Machiavellian man** (see p.28), because he's **powerful**.

4) Gertrude uses her **sexuality** to give her a hold over men, and to keep her position as **Queen**. Hamlet says she used to "**hang on**" King Hamlet (1.2.143), and her **hasty marriage** implies that she's a **weak** character.

Gertrude

Gertrude has a **Complicated Relationship** with **Hamlet**

Gertrude is pretty much the **opposite** of her son Hamlet:

Gertrude is...		Hamlet is...
• **Shallow**, and only thinks about **earthly matters**. • **Selfish** in her desires and cares about her **own pleasure**. • **Childlike** in nature — this adds to the image of her as a **victim**.		• A **scholar** and a **philosopher**, deeply **concerned** about **spiritual dilemmas**. • **Repulsed** by the **vices** of man and doesn't care for this "**mortal coil**" (3.1.67). • **Old** for his age — he's forced to confront **issues** that he's unprepared for.

Because we learn about Gertrude mostly through Hamlet's speeches, the way that Hamlet sees her has an **effect** on the way the **audience** views her. Hamlet is **obsessed** with Gertrude's **sexuality**:

1) Gertrude's **sexuality** disgusts Hamlet and leads him to turn **against her** — he says "**Frailty, thy name is woman**" (1.2.146). He's furious and horrified that she's married his uncle so **soon** after his father's death.

2) Gertrude's **incestuous marriage** leaves Hamlet thinking that the world is **contaminated**, like an "**unweeded garden**" that's "**rank and gross in nature**" (1.2.135-136). Hamlet **associates sexuality** with **sin** and **deception**.

3) Hamlet almost seems more **upset** about Gertrude's **sexual betrayal** of his father than his father's **murder**.

Some **critics** see Hamlet's attitude towards Gertrude as evidence of his **misogyny** — his **hatred** of **women**.

She could be a **Caring, Maternal Victim** or an **Adulteress Murderer**

Gertrude is usually presented as a **caring** and **maternal victim**:

1) Gertrude has **good intentions** to protect the men close to her. When she tells Claudius that Hamlet killed Polonius, she says that Hamlet "**weeps for what is done**" (4.1.27) to **protect** him.

2) Gertrude is **loving** — she remains **faithful** to Hamlet and Claudius even though their behaviour isn't **honourable**. The audience **forgives** Gertrude because she seems **kind**.

3) Her behaviour can be **childlike** and she doesn't **understand** what she's done wrong. She's **genuinely upset** when Hamlet confronts her: "**Thou turnest mine eyes into my very soul, / And there I see such black and grainèd spots**" (3.4.90-91). She suddenly realises that her actions have **tarnished** her **soul**.

The Ghost calls Claudius an "**adulterate beast**" (1.5.42), which could suggest that Gertrude and Claudius were lovers **before** the King's death. If this were the case, it could imply that she had a part in the King's **murder**. However:

1) 'Adulterate' also means 'contaminate' — the Ghost may mean that Gertrude has been contaminated **by her marriage**.

2) The Ghost says that he was "**Of life, of crown, of queen at once dispatched**" (1.5.75) — the word order suggests that he **only lost** Gertrude when he **died**. Later, in Act 3, Scene 4, Hamlet doesn't **mention** adultery when he lists her crimes. This implies that Shakespeare didn't intend to **portray** Gertrude as an adulteress.

Practice Questions

Q1 Reread Act 3, Scene 4, and write a diary entry from Gertrude's perspective, talking about the events you have just witnessed and describing how you felt about them.

Q2 "Frailty, thy name is woman." To what extent do you think Gertrude conforms to this stereotype?

"Mother, you have my father much offended"

Gertrude's ambiguity provoked much debate... Critics ranted and raved for years and years without a conclusion. Then, in 1975, Freddie Mercury wrote Bohemian Rhapsody, and revealed that "Mama just killed a man". Problem solved — hundreds of critics' lives wasted.

Ophelia

Ophelia is depicted as sweet and innocent, keen to please her father, her brother and Hamlet himself. Throughout the play Ophelia is being told what to do by the three men in her life, and she always tries to do what they ask.

Ophelia is Dependent on Men

1) There are many **parallels** between Gertrude and Ophelia. The two **main similarities** are their **naivety** and **reliance** upon men.

2) Ophelia has to rely on men even more than Gertrude because she's not as **established** in the Danish court. She has to obey her father because she's **unmarried**. Ophelia's still **young**, and her father has given her a **sheltered life**.

3) Her **language** emphasises how **subservient** she is. She receives instructions meekly: **"I shall obey, my lord"** (1.3.136) and seems to seek guidance on how she should behave: **"I do not know, my lord, what I should think"** (1.3.104).

4) Ophelia is generally **willing** to do as Polonius, Laertes and Hamlet ask — she's an affectionate person and keen to **please** them.

© CASTLE ROCK ENTERTAINMENT / THE KOBAL COLLECTION

Ophelia is Controlled by her Family

1) Ophelia is surrounded by **strong men** like Polonius and Laertes, who **control** her life.

For more on Ophelia's relationship with Polonius and Laertes, see p.34 and p.36.

- Polonius uses Ophelia as a **pawn**, ordering her to help him **spy** on Hamlet to further his **influence** with the King. Ophelia makes no attempt to **argue** or **refuse**, implying that her **duty** to her father is more **important** than her **affection** for Hamlet.

- Without a **mother** or friends to support her, Ophelia relies on her **father** for guidance. When Hamlet enters her closet **"with his doublet all unbraced"** (2.1.78), she immediately **tells Polonius**. Similarly, she shows Polonius Hamlet's **love letter**. This shows how **naive** and **trusting** she is, despite her father's distrust of her.

- She also depends on **Laertes's** advice. When he casts doubts on Hamlet's affection for her and **lectures** her on preserving her **virginity**, she doesn't attempt to **defend** herself or Hamlet, but describes it as a **"good lesson"** (1.3.45). She does **point out** that he should take his own **advice** too though.

2) Both Polonius and Laertes are **preoccupied** with Ophelia's **sexuality**. Polonius is concerned that the **"free and bounteous"** time Ophelia spends with Hamlet will damage her **"honour"** (1.3.93-97), while Laertes gives her a **long** and **graphic lecture** about the dangers of losing her **"chaste treasure"** (1.3.31).

Ophelia's Relationship with Hamlet is Complex

Unlike Gertrude, Ophelia is presented as sexually innocent.

1) Hamlet and Ophelia's relationship is a **major subplot** in the play. Ophelia's fate is **linked** to Hamlet's — his actions are the **most likely cause** of her **madness** and **death**. Both Ophelia and Hamlet show signs of madness (see p.44-45) and once Laertes finds out that Hamlet has driven her mad, his desire for **revenge** increases.

2) Despite Hamlet's aggression towards her, he seems to have once **loved** Ophelia — he wrote her a love **letter** describing his feelings and Ophelia tells Polonius that Hamlet showed her **"affection"** (1.3.98).

3) Ophelia is **heartbroken** by Hamlet's **rejection** of her in Act 3, Scene 1:

- She can't accept that Hamlet's **abuse** of her father and herself (3.1.132-141) is caused by anything other than his **madness**, and calls on the **"heavenly powers"** to **"restore him"** (3.1.142).

- She's hurt by his claim that he never loved her, saying **"I was the more deceived"** (3.1.120). She says she's **"most deject and wretched"**, because she trusted his **"music vows"** (3.1.156-157).

- She praises his **"noble mind"** and **"unmatched form"**, emphasising her **attraction** to him (3.1.151, 160).

- She seems to **forget** that Polonius and Claudius are present, and **displays** her feelings much more **openly** than usual. This highlights how **deeply** Hamlet's rejection has **hurt** her.

Ophelia

Ophelia is driven *Mad* by *Grief*

1) Unlike Hamlet's **madness**, which is at least **partly** feigned, Ophelia's madness is completely **genuine**.

2) Her descent into madness is **swift**, and is probably triggered by a **combination** of factors:

- Being left **alone** after Hamlet's and Laertes's **departures** from court.
- Hamlet's apparent **madness** and his **rejection** of her.
- Her **father's death** at the hands of the man she **loves**, and his **unceremonious** funeral.

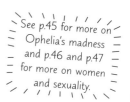
See p.45 for more on Ophelia's madness and p.46 and p.47 for more on women and sexuality.

3) **Before** her madness, she doesn't say much and appears **obedient**, **modest** and **innocent**. Her actions are controlled by **other people**. Once she goes mad, Shakespeare uses her **rambling speech** and **bawdy songs** to show a different side to her character. It's **ironic** that her madness gives her a **voice** and a **freedom** that she previously lacked.

4) Her bawdy songs could show how the pressures of **remaining chaste**, have taken their **toll** on Ophelia. She's in an impossible position — the men around her **sexualise** her, yet insist that she remains **ignorant** of sex. An alternative reading is that she was in a **sexual relationship** with Hamlet, which would explain why she sings "**Before you tumbled me, / You promised me to wed**" (4.5.63-64). Hamlet's **betrayal** would give another reason for her madness.

5) Only in her **mad speeches** and **inappropriate songs** could she be said to live up to Hamlet's **perception** of impurity. However, to everyone except Hamlet, she still seems to **symbolise purity** and virtue — Gertrude calls her "**sweet lady**" (4.5.27) and Laertes says she "**Stood challenger, on mount, of all the age / For her perfections**" (4.7.28-29).

Ophelia's *Death* raises *Questions*

1) Shakespeare doesn't make it clear to what extent Ophelia committed **suicide** or died by **accident**.

2) If she committed suicide, this **contrasts** with Hamlet, who struggles to **take action**. However, the description of Ophelia as "**incapable of her own distress**" (4.7.178) seems more in-keeping with her character — she **allows** the river to take her life, just as she previously allowed her father, brother and Hamlet to **control** her.

3) Gertrude explains that Ophelia died when she accidentally fell into the water. Gertrude's **detailed report** of Ophelia's death implies that someone was **present**, yet they didn't try to **save** Ophelia, though nobody doubts Gertrude's account. It would also be very difficult to present Ophelia drowning on stage.

4) The **description** of Ophelia's death in Act 4, Scene 7 is highly **romanticised** and **beautiful** e.g. "**mermaid-like**" (line 176). Gertrude seems to be emphasising Ophelia's **innocence** and **purity**. At Ophelia's funeral, Gertrude says she hoped Ophelia would be "**Hamlet's wife**" (5.1.240). This emphasises the **sadness** of Ophelia's death.

5) The church suspects that Ophelia committed **suicide**, and a proper funeral is **inappropriate**. The priest says that "**Her death was doubtful**" (5.1.223) and that "**Shards, flints, and pebbles should be thrown on her.**" (5.1.227).

6) Hamlet and Laertes **argue** over who loved Ophelia the most, but after her funeral scene she **isn't mentioned** again. They seem to view Ophelia as an **object** to be used to prove their **superiority**, rather than as a real person.

Practice Questions

Q1 'Ophelia is just a younger version of Gertrude.' To what extent do you agree with this analysis?

Q2 Reread Gertrude's account of Ophelia's death in Act 4, Scene 7, lines 166-183. Imagine you are a police inspector asked to investigate the circumstances of her death, and write a report describing what happened.

Q3 'Ophelia's death is the saddest event in the play.' Do you agree with this statement? Explain your answer.

"The fair Ophelia! — Nymph, in thy orisons*"

At the start of the play, Ophelia is a mild, quiet girl... but then she turns into a crazy lady who sings rude songs and makes inappropriate comments. It's not surprising that she struggles to cope — her boyfriend has just killed her father. Sad times.

*orisons = prayers

Polonius

Polonius isn't Hamlet's favourite person — when he kills him by mistake, he pretty much just shrugs and says "Oh well". Murder was probably a bit harsh, but he is very annoying... He's the Jar Jar Binks of 'Hamlet'.

Polonius is an *Incompetent Schemer*

1) As **chief advisor** to the king, Polonius is well established in the Danish court, but he seems to feel that his position is **unstable**. He hangs on to his **power** by **agreeing** with everything Claudius says and **doing** everything he asks.

2) Polonius is **knowledgeable** about courtly matters and the principles of good kingship, but struggles to **apply** his intelligence effectively. This means that he's prone to making **errors of judgment**.

3) Polonius emphasises that his advice has always been **correct** and he's never been "**proved otherwise**" (2.2.155). Essentially, it seems as if Polonius **used to be** very capable, but he's **older** and less **competent** now. He's become more of a **fool** than a counsellor.

© PARAMOUNT / THE KOBAL COLLECTION

Polonius's *Relationship* with his *Children* is *Complicated*

> The Ghost of King Hamlet is also very controlling — both fathers want their children to be obedient.

1) Polonius **acts** as if he's a **wise man** but he can't resist **childish schemes** and **deception**. Ironically his most elaborate schemes involve his two children, Laertes and Ophelia.

2) The way that Polonius talks to his superiors is **respectful** and he's **careful** about what he says. This contrasts with the way he talks to his children, e.g. he's **blunt** and **direct** when he talks to Ophelia: "**Pooh, you speak like a green girl**" (1.3.101). He doesn't feel the need to **flatter** his children in the same way he does when he's talking to others.

3) Polonius doesn't **trust** his children and tries to **control** them, but ironically it's his children who shouldn't trust him — he's **motivated** by **self interest**, not what's best for them.

Polonius and **Laertes**

1) Polonius lets Laertes **leave** Denmark, but he sends his servant Reynaldo to **spy** on him. Polonius tells Reynaldo to invent "**scandal**" (2.1.29) about Laertes — he believes that **deception** is the best way to find out information.

2) Polonius's actions here give us a **glimpse** of a **competent, sensible** man — Ophelia's comment that Laertes should avoid becoming a "**reckless libertine**" (1.3.49) hints that Polonius's suspicions are **well-founded**. His **advice** to Laertes is also very **sensible**, "**to thine own self be true**" (1.3.78).

> Contemporary Commentary
>
> It's often suggested that Polonius was **based on** Lord Burghley, a **spymaster** in Elizabeth's court, who had spied on his son in Paris. Polonius's **critical, interfering** and **self-righteous** nature is also said to be a **parody** of the **Puritans** — the Puritans **hated** the theatre, which may explain why Shakespeare made him such a **laughable** character.

Polonius and **Ophelia**

1) Polonius has a **low opinion** of Ophelia — arguably more so than any other character. Polonius believes that she's easily **corruptible** and a **liar**. He tells her to "**Give me up the truth**" (1.3.98) about her relationship with Hamlet. Ophelia replies that they've acted "**In honourable fashion**", but Polonius calls her a "**baby**" (1.3.111, 105).

2) He knows that Ophelia will do **anything** he asks, even if she does it with a heavy heart — in Elizabethan times, daughters were expected to obey their fathers. Polonius makes the most of this and **demands** that she lets him use her to spy on Hamlet. Even though she loves Hamlet, she **obeys** Polonius when he tells her not to see Hamlet again.

3) Polonius's treatment of Ophelia is **hypocritical**. He first **forbids** her from seeing Hamlet, then **orders** her to see Hamlet to **improve** Polonius's relationship with Claudius.

Polonius

He **Ruins** Hamlet and Ophelia's **Relationship**

1) When Polonius **forbids** Ophelia from seeing Hamlet, he tells her that Hamlet's vows of love are **"brokers"** (1.3.127) — he's suggesting that Hamlet is **lying** about his love for Ophelia in order to **seduce** her.

2) Polonius may be **genuinely worried** that Hamlet is lying, but an alternative explanation is that he doesn't want to **harm** his position in court — if he became Hamlet's father-in-law, Claudius might see him as a **threat**.

3) Polonius's **schemes** and **lies** make Hamlet distrust Ophelia, and lead to Polonius's death and Ophelia's madness. Polonius's **deceptive behaviour** is one of the factors that **destroys** Hamlet and Ophelia's relationship.

He **Provides** some **Comic Relief**

Although Polonius might appear **sinister**, he provides **comedy** in a **dark play**. The comedy comes from his **arrogant refusal** to consider that he might be wrong, and his **rambling**, **pompous** language:

1) His **foolish** schemes consistently **fail**, yet he never loses faith in them. His plan to use Ophelia to spy on Hamlet **backfires**, but he **immediately** starts planning his next scheme (which proves to be his **last**).

2) He's completely **insensitive** to the **situations** around him, and constantly **misjudges** them — during a moving speech made by one of the players, he **ruins** the mood by interrupting with "**This is too long**" (2.2.496). Hamlet warns the players to "**mock him not**" (2.2.541-542) — Polonius is a figure of fun to the other **characters**, as well as the audience.

3) He also misjudges **people** — he believes the only reason for Hamlet's madness is **love**, and underestimates Hamlet's hatred for Claudius. By misjudging Hamlet, his **ill-founded suspicions** lead to his **death**.

4) Polonius's speeches are so **long, self-indulgent** and **boring** that they sound ridiculous. He frequently gets **confused** to the point where the words become **meaningless**. Hamlet's sarcastic remarks show that he's **exasperated** with Polonius's rambling language, but Polonius is oblivious to Hamlet's frustration.

5) Polonius could be seen as a **parody** of Hamlet as he also often considers subjects in too much **detail** — Polonius's ability to get **lost** in his own words mirrors Hamlet's own **internal confusion**.

Polonius's **Scheming** and **Foolishness** are his own **Downfall**

1) The **murder** of Polonius is a **turning point** for Hamlet. He spends so much time **considering** his options without actually acting, but when he does **act**, it ends in **tragedy**. This highlights the **importance** of **careful thought** for Hamlet — acting on **impulse** results in the **wrong man** dying.

2) By killing Polonius, Hamlet commits the same **crime** that he was trying to punish — he has murdered a father, and put Laertes in the **same position** as himself.

3) Polonius's 'clever' **schemes** and **errors of judgment** lead to his own death. Earlier in the play, Polonius remembers that he once played Julius Caesar and was **stabbed** by the hidden conspirators. Ironically in *Hamlet*, the roles are **reversed** and Polonius, the hidden conspirator, dies.

4) Like Shakespeare's Julius Caesar, Polonius continues to **influence** events **after he dies**. His death sets off a chain reaction — Laertes's need for **vengeance** leads to the final scene in which he kills Hamlet.

Practice Questions

Q1 Polonius has been portrayed as either a blundering fool or a sinister schemer in various productions of *Hamlet*. If you were asked to play Polonius how would you portray him? Give reasons for your answer.

Q2 Write a diary entry from Ophelia's perspective, describing your feelings towards Polonius.

Q3 'Polonius has no redeeming features — he deserved to be killed.' To what extent do you agree with this analysis? Back up your answer with examples from the text.

"Thou wretched, rash, intruding fool"

Funnily enough, Hamlet said the same thing when he fell into poison ivy... except without the intruding fool bit. Unlike some of the characters in the play, Polonius is pretty straightforward — his motivations are clear and his strengths and flaws are there for all to see.

Laertes

Analysing Laertes's character is a lot like looking at a men's magazine. He likes women, sports and fast cars.
He also loves his sister. A lot. Too much. Hmmm... actually it's more like watching an episode of the Jeremy Kyle Show.

Laertes *is a* Foil *to* Hamlet

> Laertes is a 'foil' to Hamlet because he's very different but shares Hamlet's desire for revenge.

1) Shakespeare uses various **foils** to develop Hamlet's character. The main foil is Laertes, a young man also **seeking revenge** for his father's murder.

2) As **foils** for one another, Hamlet and Laertes have several things in **common**:

© Fiona Moorhead

- Hamlet and Laertes both **love Ophelia**, and have a strong sense of **love**, **loyalty** and **respect** for their fathers.
- Both are **students** studying **abroad**, well-known for their **swordsmanship**.
- They both claim to be **honourable**, but seek revenge through **devious means** — Laertes uses a **poisoned blade** and Hamlet feigns **madness**.

3) Foils also show **contrasts** between characters. When Hamlet says "**I'll be your foil, Laertes**" (5.2.252), he's modestly saying that the **difference** in their **fencing ability** will make Laertes' **skills** seem even better.

Laertes's *Actions* Contrast Sharply *with Hamlet's*

HAMLET	LAERTES
• chooses to study at the scholarly, **humanist** (p.62) university in Wittenberg.	• chooses to study in Paris so that he can lead a **hedonistic lifestyle**.
• is a **tragic hero** — he finds himself **unable** to take **revenge** for his father's death.	• is a **traditional revenge hero** (see p.42). He returns home to take revenge when he hears that his father's dead.
• is a **thinker**, but he **wishes** that he was more **impulsive**, like Laertes. However, the one time that he does act without thinking it has a **disastrous consequence** — Polonius's murder.	• is **rash** and **impulsive** but, while Hamlet **can act** on impulse, Laertes doesn't think **rationally**. He acts on his **emotions**, so he's easily **manipulated** — Claudius convinces him that vengeance is **honourable**, even if it's done deviously.
• is concerned with **spirituality** — he wants **eternal punishment**, so he refuses to kill Claudius when he's praying: "**this same villain send / To heaven. / Why, this is hire and salary**" (3.3.77-79).	• is only concerned with the **present** and has no time for **spirituality** — Laertes says he would cut Hamlet's throat "**i'th'church**" (4.7.125). He would have **taken** the opportunity to get revenge, even if Hamlet was praying.

> Hedonism is the pursuit of pleasure.

Laertes *is* Fixated *on Ophelia's Chastity*

1) Laertes loves Ophelia and is **concerned** with her wellbeing. He advises her **against** a relationship with Hamlet by saying "**Perhaps he loves you now**" (1.3.14) but that Hamlet will just **use her**. He warns her that she'll lose her "**heart, or [her] chaste treasure**" (1.3.31).

2) Despite loving his sister, he doesn't think very **highly** of her. He thinks she's likely to lose her **virginity** to Hamlet simply because he's **persistent**, and warns her that "**Youth to itself rebels, though none else near**" (1.3.44). Laertes is saying that young people are **foolish** because they are ruled by **passion** rather than rational thought.

3) When Ophelia asks if he'll follow his **own advice**, he **dismisses** her concern. This suggests that, like his father, Laertes believes in a **double standard** for men and women.

4) There are some **incestuous undertones** in Ophelia and Laertes's relationship:

- Laertes speaks to his sister in **suggestive sexual terms**. At her funeral, he **focuses** on her "**unpolluted flesh**" (5.1.235), and leaps into her grave to physically hold her: "**Hold off the earth awhile, / Till I have caught her once more in mine arms**" (5.1.245-246).
- His **argument** with Hamlet is over who loved her the **most** — they sound like **love rivals**.
- It's been suggested that Laertes suspected Hamlet of **corrupting** Ophelia's chastity — if he did have **incestuous desire** for his sister, this would have provoked **anger** and **jealousy**.

Laertes

Laertes's *Language Echoes* his *Father's*

1) Laertes's language is **similar** to Polonius's — he uses the same pompous **tone** and **abuses words** in a similar way. Whereas Polonius is fond of **rambling complexities**, Laertes uses **exaggeration** to put his point across.

2) Laertes's similarity to his father can be seen in Act 1, Scene 3 where Laertes's **long, preachy** speech to Ophelia is followed by an almost **identical** one made by Polonius. The speeches are similar in **content** and **style** — they both call Hamlet's feelings a passing "**fashion**" (lines 6 & 112).

3) Laertes's **exaggerated language** is most obvious at Ophelia's funeral, where he uses numbers to **emphasise** his grief: "**treble woe / Fall ten times double**" (5.1.242-243). By exaggerating his sorrow like this, Laertes's numerical language actually sounds **hollow** and **unfeeling**.

4) Hamlet **mocks** Laertes's hyperbole (exaggeration) because he thinks it makes Laertes sound **insincere**: "**Forty thousand brothers / Could not with all their quantity of love / Make up my sum**" (5.1.265-267).

Laertes thinks *Appearances* are *More Important* than *Substance*

1) Polonius's best advice to his son is "**to thine own self be true**" (1.3.78). Despite what Polonius says, he's really more **concerned** about how Laertes **appears** than who he actually **is**, and he's passed this **attitude** on to Laertes.

2) Laertes appears more **upset** that his father didn't get a **nobleman's funeral** than the fact that he was **murdered**. He **complains** that the funeral was "**obscure**" (4.5.213) — his family's **social position** is very important to him.

3) Laertes's **anger** at Ophelia's funeral is also partly the result of his preoccupation with **appearances**. He asks "**Must there no more be done**?" (5.1.231) — he wants Ophelia to have a grand funeral, despite the fact that her death was "**doubtful**" (5.1.23) and the church had already made a **concession** by giving her a **Christian burial**.

Fortinbras is a *Mix* of *Laertes* and *Hamlet*

1) Fortinbras is a **foil** to Laertes and Hamlet. He's placed in **similar circumstances** as his father was killed (Fortinbras's father was killed in combat by King Hamlet), but he seeks vengeance in a **different way** from Hamlet and Laertes. If Laertes is the **opposite** of Hamlet, Fortinbras is more a **mixture** of the two.

2) Like Laertes, Fortinbras is **actively** seeking revenge. He initially plans to attack Denmark, but changes his mind on advice from his uncle (the King of Norway). This shows that although he can be **rash**, he's also capable of acting in a **reasoned manner**. He appears to have the ability to **reason** *and* **act** — the fact that Shakespeare has him **succeed**, whilst Hamlet and Laertes **die**, suggests that Shakespeare felt that both traits are equally **important**.

3) Hamlet has a **major turning point** when he compares himself to Fortinbras. Hamlet is **ashamed** that he hasn't taken vengeance on his **guilty** uncle, whilst Fortinbras is prepared to do battle and **sacrifice** men's lives over an "**eggshell**" (4.4.53). Hamlet decides that, "**from this time forth / My thoughts be bloody, or be nothing worth**" (4.4.65-66).

4) The play's **resolution** highlights Fortinbras's **positive traits**. When he arrives in Elsinore he quickly **assesses** the situation, then **acts** upon it. When Fortinbras is named king, the play comes **full circle** — his father's lost lands are **returned** and the **corrupt court** is **dead** at his feet. Denmark is **no longer rotten**.

Practice Questions

Q1 Write a summary of how you imagine Denmark would have been under: a) Hamlet   b) Fortinbras
Decide whether Fortinbras or Hamlet would have made the better king.

Q2 'If Hamlet had been more like Laertes, there would have been less bloodshed.'
To what extent do you agree with this statement?

Q3 Which character is the most heroic — Hamlet, Laertes or Fortinbras? Give reasons for your answer.

"In my terms of honour / I stand aloof, and will no reconcilement"

Laertes pretty much exists to act as a foil to Hamlet. Horatio's the cling-film, sticking with Hamlet no matter what, Ophelia's the baking paper — she might have a bun in the oven, and Fortinbras is the kitchen roll, he comes and clears up the mess at the end...

Horatio

Hooray for Horatio! He's pretty much the only good guy in the whole play. Everyone else has lots of problems and flaws. Unfortunately, he's not the most exciting bloke — nice guys rarely are. It's the screwed up ones that are the most interesting.

Horatio is Hamlet's Only Ally

1) Horatio is Hamlet's **closest friend**. Unlike Rosencrantz and Guildenstern, Horatio is consistently **loyal** and **trustworthy** throughout the play.

2) Horatio's loyalty is shown most clearly when he offers to **commit suicide** and **die alongside** Hamlet in Act 5, Scene 2.

3) He's the **only person** who remains **close** to Hamlet in spite of the prince's **isolation**. All of Hamlet's relationships are **damaged**, except his friendship with Horatio. Horatio is **"one man picked out of ten thousand"** who is honest (2.2.178-9) because he's the only person who isn't **affected** by the **corruption** in the court.

4) Hamlet's **conversations** with Horatio, alongside his **soliloquies**, give the best **insights** we have into Hamlet's character.

© CASTLE ROCK ENTERTAINMENT / THE KOBAL COLLECTION / KONOW, ROLF

Hamlet Admires Horatio's Self-control

Being stoic means emphasising reason and duty over emotion.

1) Hamlet **admires** Horatio for having the qualities that he **lacks**. He praises Horatio for his **virtue**, **self-control** and **stoic attitude** and wishes that he could have a similar state of mind: **"Give me that man / That is not passion's slave, and I will wear him / In my heart's core"** (3.2.81-83).

2) In this quote, Hamlet seems almost **envious** of Horatio's **freedom** from **emotion**, however Horatio is not completely **unfeeling**. He does have a strong **love** for Hamlet, but he never lets it **control** him.

3) Even when Horatio offers to **commit suicide** for Hamlet, he's **level-headed** and **calm**, motivated by a sense of **honour** and **duty**. He calls himself **"more an antique Roman than a Dane"** (5.2.335). This links his character to the values of the **Classical world** where suicide was considered **heroic** in some circumstances.

4) Horatio is **calm**, **thoughtful** and speaks only when **necessary**. In comparison, Hamlet's speeches are **frequent** and **meandering**, and his emotions **delay** his vengeance.

5) Hamlet wants to **learn** from Horatio's stoic attitude — he wishes that he could be more **rational** and **indifferent to fortune**. By the end of the play, Hamlet has **accepted his fate**: **"There's a divinity that shapes our ends"** (5.2.10).

He has an Important Dramatic Function

Horatio's name sounds like 'orator', the Latin for 'speaker', and in Greek Horatio means 'guardian'.

Horatio's role in the plot is quite **minor** but he has an important **dramatic purpose**:

1) Shakespeare uses Horatio in a role similar to the chorus to **help** shape the audience's **experience** of the play. Horatio introduces the idea that the play is full of **doubt** and **ambiguity** from the **start** by refusing to believe in the Ghost: **"Horatio says 'tis but our fantasy"** (1.1.23).

2) As a **self-reflexive** play, *Hamlet* deliberately draws attention to the fact that it's a staged production by referring to techniques of the theatre — in this case that **Horatio** is like the **chorus**. The chorus was a device used in **Classical Greek** plays to **narrate** the story and **comment** on the dramatic **action**.

3) Shakespeare **deliberately** doesn't give Horatio much of a role in the play's **events** because it **helps** to establish his **chorus-like function** — Horatio only speaks when he has something **important** to say.

4) When Horatio does speak, he's frequently **sceptical** or **critical** of the events taking place. Hamlet is often **headstrong** about his beliefs, but Horatio remains **impartial** — he doesn't necessarily **believe** the Ghost was King Hamlet, and he's **noncommittal** about whether Hamlet's play **proved** Hamlet's suspicions about Claudius.

5) As an **observer** of the play's events, Horatio grounds the play in **reality**. He makes it **easier** for the audience to see what's **real** and what's not, because he's part of the action. Horatio **believes** that Hamlet is merely feigning madness so, without Horatio, Hamlet's **sanity** would be more **uncertain**.

6) Horatio survives to tell Hamlet's **story** — he promises to tell **"th'yet unknowing world / How these things came about"** (5.2.373-374), though the play ends before he actually does this. By being involved in the **action** and by never talking **directly** to the audience, Horatio's role is different from a conventional **chorus**.

Rosencrantz and Guildenstern

I'm going to be super ambitious and deal with two characters in one page. Rosencrantz is an old friend of Hamlet's, dishonest but incompetent, whilst Guildenstern is an old friend of Hamlet's, dishonest but incompetent — this might not be so difficult...

They're Interchangeable Characters

1) Rosencrantz and Guildenstern only ever appear **together** and seem **incapable** of functioning **independently**. They talk in a **similar** way and **finish** each other's sentences. Gertrude's repetition of Claudius's line "**Thanks Rosencrantz, and gentle Guildenstern**" (2.2.33) with the names **reversed** implies that it's difficult to tell them apart.

2) Their names are also **similar**. Both have three syllables, and both share the same **syllabic emphasis**.

Tom Stoppard wrote a play based around these characters called Rosencrantz and Guildenstern Are Dead. In Stoppard's play even the two characters can't tell each other apart.

3) They can be seen as **deception personified** — their two-faced nature shows that friendship is not for **life** and that loyalty can be **bought**.

Rosencrantz and Guildenstern contrast with Horatio, who is absolutely loyal to Hamlet.

They're Dishonest, but not very Bright

1) Their names have **Christian symbolism** which is ironic because they aren't very **moral** characters — Rosencrantz means '**Crown of roses**' (or thorns) and Guildenstern means '**Golden star**'. They ignore the Christian values of **love** and **friendship** and instead **betray** Hamlet for their own **profit**.

2) However, they're not very good at **deception** — Hamlet **immediately realises** that they're working for Claudius. This provides some **humour** in the play as they act like **fools** and serve as comic **foils** to Hamlet's wit.

3) The characters seem out of their **depth** and have **no control** over their own **destiny** or the **events** of the play itself. They believe their "**indifferent**" lives are due to **fate**: "**On Fortune's cap we are not the very button**" (2.2.227, 229).

4) Their **deaths** are a result of a plot which they don't **understand**. In Stoppard's play the pair also find themselves in a drama that they can't **comprehend**, which mirrors their situation in *Hamlet*.

Rosencrantz and Guildenstern are Dead, but Nobody Cares

1) Their deaths reveal the **complicated nature** of Hamlet's **character**. He's **incapable** of taking revenge on his **deserving** uncle, yet he's **able** to send his old **friends** to their **deaths** without a second thought, simply shrugging off responsibility: "**They are not near my conscience**" (5.2.58).

2) The pair might not have been particularly **loyal**, but their deaths do seem **unjustified**. They were **unaware** of the contents of Claudius's letter and it's **unclear** how deep their betrayal of Hamlet was — it's possible that they were only following Claudius's orders out of **fear**.

3) Hamlet had **warned** the pair, "**you cannot play upon me**" (3.2.379), suggesting that they couldn't hope to **understand** or **affect** his actions (and by extension the events of the play). Perhaps Hamlet felt that they **deserved** their fate because they show such **greed** or **stupidity**, and don't listen to his warnings.

Practice Questions

Q1 'The characters of Rosencrantz and Guildenstern add nothing to the play — *Hamlet* could have easily done without them.' To what extent do you agree with this statement?

Q2 What do you think is more important — Horatio's function as the play's chorus, or his role as Hamlet's only true friend?

Q3 Imagine that you are Horatio, and are describing the events of Elsinore to Fortinbras. Write a short summary of *Hamlet*, making sure that you maintain Horatio's characteristics (stoic, reasoned, critical etc).

"In this harsh world draw thy breath in pain, / To tell my story"

Horatio can be quite difficult to get your head around — he's in the play but he's also an observer of the play... It's all very confusing, but it's quite an important idea. It would be so much easier if he was just a simple fool like Rosencrantz and Guildenstern.

The Ghost

I actually played the Ghost in my school production of 'Hamlet'. It was all going swimmingly until a red sock snuck into the washing machine — it's pretty hard to terrify anybody when you're just running around dressed in a pink sheet...

King Hamlet was a Good King

Though we only see King Hamlet as a **Ghost**, there's a lot of **evidence** to suggest what **kind of man** he was:

© 2005 TopFoto

1) Under King Hamlet, Denmark was **honourable** and **respected**. Horatio describes him as a **noble king** who ruled in the interests of his **kingdom**.

2) He was a **brave** and "**valiant**" (1.1.84) **warrior**, who ably **defended** his country against **invasion**. He also killed Old Fortinbras in **single combat**, gaining **land** for Denmark and providing **stability** during his reign.

3) He was a "**loving**" (1.2.140) husband to Gertrude, and even after death he's **considerate** towards her — he tells Hamlet to "**step between her and her fighting soul!**" (3.4.114) because he wants Hamlet to **help** Gertrude.

4) Shakespeare gives father and son the **same** name to suggest that they had **similar characteristics**. King Hamlet's an **ideal king**, and Fortinbras believes that Hamlet would "**have proved most royal**" (5.2.392) if he'd had the chance to rule.

5) The Ghost and Hamlet also **talk alike**, particularly when they refer to Gertrude's marriage. In Act 2, Scene 1 they even **look alike** — Ophelia says Hamlet is "**Pale... As if he had been loosèd out of hell**" (2.1.81-83).

Shakespeare Uses the Ghost in an Unusual Way

1) **Revenge tragedies** (see p.42) such as *Hamlet* **commonly** featured ghosts. Murder victims in revenge tragedies would visit their relatives to ask them to seek **revenge**, so the Ghost in *Hamlet* isn't unusual.

2) However, it is unusual that the Ghost provokes so much **speculation**. The **uncertainty** over the **Ghost** and its **message** suggests that this isn't a **standard** revenge tragedy but a complicated **psychological dilemma**.

3) Hamlet vows to avenge his father's death "**with wings as swift / As meditation or the thoughts of love**" (1.5.29-30). The Ghost doesn't seem to doubt that Hamlet will fulfil his promise: "**I find thee apt**" (1.5.31). This could suggest that he doesn't have the ability to see into the **future**, as Hamlet **struggles** to take **action**.

The Ghost's Origin and Message are Uncertain

> Catholics believe that purgatory is a place where souls undergo a temporary period of suffering to be purified of their sins.

1) The Ghost **tells Hamlet** that:

- He's Hamlet's **father** — Horatio and the guards all confirm that he **resembles** the dead king.
- He was **murdered** by Claudius and he's "**Doomed**" (1.5.10) to suffer in "**sulphurous and tormenting flames**" (1.5.3) until the "**foul crimes done in my days of nature / Are burnt and purged away**" (1.5.12-13).
- Hamlet must "**Revenge his foul and most unnatural murder**" (1.5.25) so that he can escape purgatory.

2) The Ghost's message seems fairly **straightforward**, but his speech is actually full of **confusing contradictions**:

- At first he **rejects** Hamlet's pity but the **violent description** of his **torment** inevitably provokes such a reaction.
- He **draws attention** to Gertrude's **betrayal** in **vivid language** but then tells Hamlet not to think about it.
- He complains about the **immorality** of killing a **king** who's also a **relative**, before asking Hamlet to do the **same**.

3) There's also uncertainty over **who** the Ghost is. He could be the Ghost of **Hamlet's father**, but his demands aren't particularly **fatherly** — he doesn't seem to **care** about his son's **fate** as long as he's **avenged**.

- It's possible that he's a **demon** — his motives appear to be **malicious**.
- He could be a **manifestation** of Hamlet's grief. The Ghost might just be a **representation** of the fact that Hamlet is **haunted** by his father's **memory**. The way he echoes Hamlet's inner thoughts could **support** this.
- The Ghost's **armour** is a reminder that Denmark is in **grave danger** from Fortinbras, so he could **embody** Denmark's **growing social unrest** at the prospect of war.

The Ghost

The Ghost is an important Dramatic Device

The Ghost serves a variety of **purposes** within the play:

1) The play **opens** with the sentinels and Horatio discussing the Ghost. Francisco and Barnardo are **nervous**, which creates an atmosphere of **fear** and **uncertainty**. When the Ghost appears he **doesn't speak**, which builds **suspense**.

2) The Ghost **foreshadows** the tragedy to come. Horatio wonders if it **"bodes some strange eruption to our state"** (1.1.69) and compares its presence to the strange **portents** that occurred before **Julius Caesar's death**. The Ghost therefore suggests to both the characters and the audience that some **tragedy** is about to occur.

3) Horatio also suspects the Ghost may have some **supernatural knowledge** of the "country's fate" (1.1.134) which could save Denmark. This reminds the audience of the likelihood of **war**, and builds **tension**.

4) The Ghost's demands on Hamlet **drive** his actions, so it acts as a device to **move** the plot **forward**. It also leads to Hamlet's moral and psychological **torment**, which defines his **character** and forms the **basis** of the play.

5) Shakespeare uses the Ghost to **reveal** Hamlet's **innermost thoughts**. When the Ghost tells Hamlet that Claudius murdered him, Hamlet replies **"O my prophetic soul!"** (1.5.40), suggesting that he already **suspected** this.

6) The **nature** and **purpose** of the Ghost are never resolved. This adds to the sense that nothing is certain, and everything is open to **interpretation**.

The Ghost Challenges Hamlet's Religious Beliefs

1) Denmark is a **Protestant country**, and Hamlet studies in Wittenberg, the home of the Protestant **Reformation**. Protestants **don't believe** in purgatory, so the Ghost's claims **challenge** Hamlet's religious **faith**. Hamlet questions whether it's a "**spirit of health or goblin damned**" (1.4.40) but the answer remains unclear.

2) **Stephen Greenblatt** argues that the Ghost represents a widespread **fear** of being **forgotten** after death. The turn of the **sixteenth century** was a time of **religious uncertainty** — the Reformation **didn't accept** the traditional Catholic idea of purgatory. Hamlet's struggle to **reconcile** his own Protestant beliefs with the Ghost's claims can be seen as **symbolising** the struggle between the **conflicting faiths** of Catholicism and Protestantism.

The Ghost's Ambiguity Delays Hamlet's Revenge

1) Though the Ghost sets the **revenge plot** in **motion**, Hamlet's uncertainty about it **delays** the play's action. Hamlet lives in a world of constant ambiguity and the Ghost **symbolises** this — even the **traditional revenge plot** is uncertain.

2) From the moment Hamlet **confronts** the spirit, he is never **sure of himself** — what he **believes** in one scene, he **doubts** in the next. Hamlet thinks he **knows** that "**It is an honest ghost**" (1.5.138) but as soon as he's alone, Hamlet is full of doubt and fear: "**The spirit that I have seen / May be a devil**" (2.2.596-597).

3) Hamlet's action is **delayed** by his **doubts**, and he's influenced by Horatio who's also **sceptical** about the Ghost. Horatio wants **proof** that the Ghost is telling the **truth**. It could be said that Hamlet would have been mad to kill his uncle **before** he was certain, and that feigning madness was **necessary** to **confirm** his suspicions.

Practice Questions

Q1 Make a list of the evidence from the play for the Ghost being:
a) Hamlet's dead father   b) A demon   c) The embodiment of Denmark's social unrest
Decide which explanation is the most convincing, giving reasons for your answer.

Q2 Reread Act 1, Scene 1 and Scene 4. Write an account of the Ghost's appearances from Marcellus's perspective.

Q3 'Without the Ghost, there would be no play.' To what extent do you agree with this statement?

"Thou comest in such a questionable shape"

The Ghost brings more problems than answers — before it came along, Hamlet was as happy as Larry... well, not really, but he was certainly less confused. Shakespeare could have made Hamlet's life much easier if he'd just got the Ghost to go 'Wooooooohhh!'

Revenge

Take two handfuls of bitter acrimony and stir in a good helping of blood. Allow to simmer, adding a pinch of the supernatural to taste. Fold into a casing of false identity or madness and allow to set. Revenge is a dish best served cold.

Revenge *was seen as an* Old *and* Unlawful *kind of* Justice

1) In Shakespeare's time, the Church taught that **revenge** was a **sin** — it was wrong for a man to settle disputes himself. The Bible says that revenge is God's **responsibility**: "Vengeance [is] **mine**" (Romans 12:19).

> • This explains why Hamlet wonders if the **ghost** of his father is the **"devil"** in a **"pleasing shape"** (2.2.597-598) because it **tempts** him to commit the **sin** of **revenge**.
>
> • The Ghost's **appearance** would have **contradicted** the **Protestant Church's** teachings (see p.41). Hamlet has to decide whether to follow his **beliefs** or the **Ghost's orders**.

2) In contrast, **classical traditions** supported revenge if there was **family honour** at stake. Revenge plays by **Seneca**, a **Stoic** philosopher from the **Roman** times, **punished villains** in a way that matched their crimes.

3) The conflict between **Christian values** and the **duty** of **blood revenge** became a common theme in Elizabethan **theatre**. This may have been because **religious** upheaval during the period made people **question** their beliefs.

Revenge Tragedy *was a* Popular Dramatic Genre

1) Elizabethan playwrights were influenced by **Seneca's** dramas from the 1st century. They started to write **bloody** and **violent** plays that followed a similar **structure**:

> i) **murder** — usually of an **important** and **innocent** person, e.g. a king or a lover.
>
> ii) **supernatural vision** — a **ghost** that makes the revenger accept their **duty**.
>
> iii) **planning** — the revenger prepares a **punishment** designed to **fit** the **crime**. This period of planning often involves a **disguise** or **madness**, either **real** or **feigned**.
>
> iv) **violence** — the revenger carries out their planned **attack**.
>
> v) **annihilation** — the play ends in a blood bath. Most of the major characters die, including the revenger whose death **restores** the **balance** and **ends** the **bloodshed**.

2) Modern scholars call plays that share these **characteristics 'revenge tragedies'**.

> **Thomas Kyd's *The Spanish Tragedy***
>
> Thomas Kyd's *The Spanish Tragedy* was **popular** in the late 16th century and **established** the revenge tragedy **genre**. It shows a **corrupt court** where the protagonist, Hieronimo, takes revenge into his **own hands**. When he shouts "**Vindicta mihi!**", he's quoting from the book of Romans in the Latin Bible, "**Vengeance [is] mine**".

Hamlet's *not a* Typical Revenger

1) Shakespeare was **influenced** by *The Spanish Tragedy*. However, instead of creating another **blood-thirsty** revenger, Shakespeare's Hamlet is an **anxious**, **hesitant thinker**. Hamlet could be seen as a **humanist** revenger.

> **Renaissance Humanism**
>
> The Protestant Reformation coincided with the rise of **humanism** — a school of thought which believed that **studying** philosophy, reason and ethics, like Hamlet's education in **Wittenberg**, led to **well-rounded** individuals. They were interested in the human **experience** and man's **ability** to **understand** the world.

Humanism was a kind of cultural 'reformation' that still influences culture today. For more about humanism, see p.48 and p.62.

2) **Stephen Greenblatt** notes that humanists turned a person's **thoughts** into an important part of their **identity**. Hamlet's **need** for **revenge** is **compromised** because he's so **influenced** by his thoughts. He's more concerned with how he **feels** on the **inside** rather than with his **duty** to seek revenge.

Revenge

Hamlet thinks that it's his **Fate** to take **Revenge**

1) Hamlet's **language** repeatedly suggests that it's his **fate** to become a **revenger**.

- Hamlet tells the Ghost that he's **"bound to hear"** his story. The Ghost focuses on the word **"bound"** when he replies **"So art thou to revenge, when thou shalt hear"** (1.5.6-7). The Ghost makes it clear that **learning** the **truth** about his murder is **equivalent** to being **duty-bound** to avenge it.
- Hamlet suggests that the only reason he **exists** is to restore **order** to the state of Denmark: **"The time is out of joint. O, cursèd spite, / That ever I was born to set it right!"** (1.5.188-189).

2) However, throughout the play, Hamlet **tests** his **role** as revenger and **resists** his **given** role:

- Hamlet believes that he can **"Rough-hew"** his own destiny, even though he acknowledges the **power** and **role** of fate: **"There's a divinity that shapes our ends"** (5.2.10-11).
- In Act 3, Scene 1, Hamlet **weighs** up whether it's better to **suffer** what **fate** brings or to be **responsible** for his own actions: **"to take arms against a sea of troubles / And by opposing end them"** (3.1.59-60). The **position** of this soliloquy at the play's **centre** makes it an important **turning point** for Hamlet.
- When Hamlet has time to **think**, he chooses to **delay** his revenge. He could have **killed** Claudius while he's **praying** in Act 3 — Hamlet says **"And now I'll do't"** (3.3.74), but lets the moment **pass**.

3) The **relationship** between **fate** and **free will** is left **deliberately ambiguous**. The audience must decide whether they think Hamlet is **predestined** to take revenge or whether he's **free** to **decide** his own **future**.

To **Act** or not to Act — that is the **Problem**...

1) *Hamlet* is defined by its **lack** of **action**. The play is considered to share the **structure** of other revenge tragedies but Shakespeare **shifts** the **focus** from the revenger's obsessive **planning** to Hamlet's **indecision**.

2) Hamlet tries to **encourage** himself to act by using more **violent** and **determined** language:

- After seeing Claudius's **reaction** to the players' performance in Act 3, Hamlet is so angry that he says **"Now could I drink hot blood"** (3.2.397) and declares he will **"speak daggers"** (3.2.403) to his mother. The play-within-a-play is a **characteristic feature** of revenge tragedy, and at this point in the play Hamlet's **language** becomes more like a **revenger's** — yet he still doesn't **do** anything.
- Just before Hamlet leaves for England he admits that he's frustrated with himself for his lack of **action** and compares himself to Fortinbras whose **"divine ambition"** (4.4.49) motivates him to fight. This leads him to **promise** that **"from this time forth, / My thoughts be bloody, or be nothing worth"** (4.4.65-66).

3) Hamlet's **"thoughts"** are the **problem** as he cannot **act** until he **stops thinking**. Just after he finally kills Claudius, he tells Horatio **"I am dead"** (5.2.327). This shows that he was **already dying** when he killed Claudius — he acts **impulsively** because he has **nothing** more to **lose**.

4) There are a few revenge plots in the play — Hamlet, Laertes and Fortinbras all want revenge for their **fathers' deaths**. Hamlet **contrasts** with Laertes and Fortinbras, because they **actively** seek revenge (see p.36-37).

Practice Questions

Q1   Reread Act 1, Scene 5, lines 1-112. To what extent and in what way is Hamlet "bound" to revenge after this scene?

Q2   'Hamlet is not really a revenger. He is a philosopher.' Do you agree with this statement? Explain your answer using evidence from the play.

Q3   "Be thou a spirit of health or goblin damned" (1.4.40). Discuss the ways in which Hamlet's religious beliefs complicate his desire for revenge.

"Revenge his foul and most unnatural murder"

Don't think you can 'do a Hamlet' and get out of this. You've got your work cut out and if you dally around too long, the deadline will pass. True, you're trying to learn about 'Hamlet', not wreak bloody revenge in the king's court. But still, get on with it — revise.

ing (1.2.20) but **only** the revenger notices, they might feel as if they're the only **sane** person and everyone else is **mad**.

Madness

If you think that you can tell a hawk from a handsaw, or a raven from a writing desk, or a budgie from a stapler then you're about as sane as Hamlet is not. Or as sane as he pretends to be. Oh, it's enough to make you mad...

Revengers sometimes **Pretend** to be **Mad**

1) In revenge tragedies, the revenger often **fakes madness** to help him carry out his plan without **arousing suspicion**.

> **Madness as a revenge strategy**
>
> In Shakespeare's **first** tragedy, *Titus Andronicus,* Titus is duty-bound to **avenge** his daughter Lavinia's **rape** and **mutilation**. He **pretends** to be **mad** so that Tamora, the mother of Lavinia's attackers, will let her **guard down**. Titus is then able to **capture** Tamora's **sons** and **kill** them.

2) However, **madness** can also be a **reaction** to a world 'gone mad'. If the world is "**disjoint and out of frame**" (1.2.20) but **only** the revenger notices, they might feel as if they're the only **sane** person and everyone else is **mad**.

> **Madness as a result of grief**
>
> In Thomas Kyd's *The Spanish Tragedy,* Hieronimo and his wife find their son **hanged**, making them both **mad** with **grief**. However, they feign **sanity** in order to **convince** their enemies to put on a **play**, during which they **stab** them and then commit **suicide**. Here, **sanity** is a **device** for **revenge**.

Hamlet's **Madness** might be an **Act**...

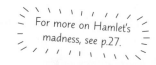

For more on Hamlet's madness, see p.27.

1) Hamlet seems to be **planning** his madness when he **warns** his friends that he'll "**put an antic disposition on**" (1.5.172) — this suggests he's going to **adopt mad behaviour** to pursue his plans for revenge.

2) Ophelia describes him as having his "**doublet all unbraced**" and his "**head thus waving up and down**" (2.1.78-93) which makes his madness seem more like a **performance** because he shows such **exaggerated symptoms**.

3) Hamlet's language is **calculated**. What appears to be **nonsense** is actually a set of well-crafted **insults**. Polonius notices that "**this be madness, yet there is method in't**" (2.2.205-206) and Claudius **suspects** Hamlet "**puts on this confusion**" (3.1.2):

> Hamlet pretends to describe himself as a **toothless**, "**wrinkled**" old man who has no "**wit**" (2.2.197-201). Hamlet adds that Polonius will be this old "**if, like a crab, you could go backward**" (2.2.204). This **turns** it into an **insult** because it suggests Polonius will have to go 'back' in time to be Hamlet's age. Of course, Polonius is the **old** man that Hamlet described.

© Donald Cooper/Rex Features

...or **Depression** and **Stress** may have made him **Mad**

1) At some points in the play Hamlet seems genuinely **distressed**. In his first soliloquy he contemplates **suicide**, saying that he'd prefer to **die** if "**self-slaughter**" (1.2.131-2) wasn't a **sin**. The Ghost's message puts more **pressure** on Hamlet because it forces Hamlet to **question** his **beliefs** and **commit to killing** Claudius.

2) The audience **never sees** Hamlet before his father's **death** so it's **hard** to know what Hamlet's normally like. Hamlet isn't **sure** of his **mental state** either. The **longer** he **acts mad**, the **more** he seems to **lose grip** on **reality**:

> In Act 5, Scene 1, Hamlet warns Laertes that he has in him "**something dangerous, / Which let thy wisdom fear**" (5.1.258-259). He could either be filled with a **rage** that threatens his **sanity** or he could be in such a **mad passion** that Laertes would be 'wise' to **avoid** getting into a **fight** with him. Either way, he acts so **strangely** that Gertrude calls it "**mere madness**" (5.1.281).

3) In the **final scene**, Hamlet **declares** that he was **really mad**. He talks in the **third person**, dividing himself into the **mad Hamlet** and the **sane Hamlet**: "**His madness is poor Hamlet's enemy**" (5.2.233). Adopting a 'split' personality could be a way for Hamlet to **express** his **confusing emotions** or a way to **explain** his **behaviour**.

Madness

Like Hamlet, **Ophelia** is **Distressed** by her father's **Death**

1) Polonius's death **disturbs** Ophelia — the King calls her madness "**the poison of deep grief**" (4.5.76). It's made worse by the fact that Polonius was killed by the **man** she **loved**, and that his burial was done **quickly** and **secretly**, in "**hugger-mugger**" (4.5.85), while her brother's away and unable to defend the family's **honour**.

2) Ophelia falls into a different kind of **madness** from Hamlet's "**antic disposition**" (1.5.172):

   - Unlike Hamlet's **witty quips** disguised as **nonsense**, Ophelia's "**speech is nothing**" (4.5.7) and marked by "**half sense**" (4.5.7). She **rambles** and **sings** bits of **folk songs** with **bawdy** undertones.

   - She has lost all **self-consciousness** and the **ability** to act **appropriately** in the **public court**. This contrasts with Hamlet's **private** display of **madness** in both Ophelia's and Gertrude's **closet**.

   - Ophelia's **death** is **troubling** for several reasons:

     1) The fact that Ophelia's death happens **offstage** means that the **audience** aren't sure whether she committed **suicide**. If she did, she **managed** to do what Hamlet could only think about.

     2) Ophelia may have been so **distressed** by **grief** that she didn't **care** that she was **drowning**.

     3) It seems **strange** that Ophelia's death was apparently **witnessed** but it wasn't **prevented**. However, it would have been **difficult** to show a drowning **on stage**. For more, see p.33.

Ophelia's **Madness** seems **Genuine**

1) Ophelia's insanity may be a good **contrast** to Hamlet's madness as they're both **grieving** for **murdered fathers**. By comparing the two characters, the audience realises that Ophelia is genuinely mad while Hamlet's sanity is more ambiguous.

2) However, Ophelia's **bawdy** songs suggest that there's **more** to her **madness** than **grief**. She sings a song to the king that's overtly **sexual** and inappropriate for a young, unmarried woman:

Women were often seen as either chaste or promiscuous (see p.32) — if a woman had sex out of marriage, she was considered worthless.

   - Ophelia sings about the "**Young men**" (4.5.61) who will **promise** to **marry** a woman in order to have **sex** with her but then **break** their **promise** as soon as they "**come to [their] bed**" (4.5.67). This would have been a **cruel trick** to play on a **young woman**, whose **reputation** would have been **ruined**.

   - The **sexual content** of her songs shows that she's **preoccupied** with **sexuality** and is voicing it in an **inappropriate** way. This suggests that she **knows more** about **sex** than a **chaste woman** should.

   - Ophelia's songs could be the result of the **pressure** from society to be **chaste**. Ophelia's **madness** gives her a **voice** and **control** over her **body** — for the **first time** she isn't being **controlled** by the men in her life. This contrasts with Ophelia's behaviour in Act 1, Scene 3 when she says to Polonius "**I do not know my lord, what I should think**" (1.3.104).

3) Ophelia's **madness** is genuine and **rooted** in **painful experiences**. She's **trapped** in a **lonely life** in Elsinore, her **father** and **brother control** her life and **Hamlet's discarded** her.

Practice Questions

Q1 "I am but mad north-north-west. When the wind is southerly, I know a hawk from a handsaw" (2.2.377-378). Analyse this quotation in the context of Hamlet's use of madness as a revenge tactic.

Q2 Read Act 2, Scene 1, lines 75-100. Rewrite this as an extra scene that shows Hamlet and Ophelia in the closet together.

Q3 'In *Hamlet*, the real tragedy is Ophelia's madness.' To what extent do you agree with this statement?

"Madness in great ones must not unwatched go"

Don't spend too long worrying about whether Hamlet was really mad. Just remember that his mental state was unusually ambiguous. Ophelia's madness isn't in doubt — she's madder than Mad Jack McMad, the winner of this year's Mr Madman competition.

Gender and Sexuality

The play's men and women may all live together in Elsinore, but the roles of gender and the dangers of sexuality keep them apart. You could say Shakespeare's play has a sexual a-gender... but you wouldn't because it makes no sense.

Gender played an Important role in Elizabethan Society

1) In Elizabethan society, **men** were more **powerful** and **privileged** than the **women** of their own **class**.

> **Men**
> - Eldest sons **inherited** their father's **estate**. A daughter only inherited if she was an **unmarried, only child**.
> - It was **common** for men to visit **brothels** without much **damage** to their **reputation**.
> - However, **syphilis** was a **widespread disease** passed on through sex. Laertes warns Ophelia of the "**Contagious blastments**" (1.3.42) that could affect **reckless** lovers. This could refer to the **physical symptoms** of the **disease** or the **corruption** of her **innocence** by men's **sexual desires**.

2) **Women** were considered to be **socially, intellectually** and **physically inferior** to men. However, the monarch for most of Shakespeare's life was **Queen Elizabeth I**, who was well-known to be a **fiercely intelligent woman**.

> **Women**
> - It was still an **accepted idea** that all women, since **Eve** in the Bible, were **responsible** for humanity's **fall** into **evil**. Since classical times, women had been considered to be '**faulty**' versions of men.
> - Women had to be **virgins** before **marriage** to ensure their children were legitimate — men needed to make sure that any **property** was **inherited** by their **biological sons** and not **illegitimate heirs**.
> - It wasn't **socially acceptable** for a **woman** to have an **affair**. If a woman was unfaithful, she made a '**cuckold**' of her husband, represented by a man with **horns** — like the **devil** or a **monster**. Hamlet refers to this when he says to Ophelia: "**marry a fool. For wise men know well enough what monsters you make of them**" (3.1.138-140).

In 'Hamlet' Gender Restricts the way the characters Live...

1) In the 16th century, women and men were thought to have **gender-specific** weaknesses:

> **Feminine Flaws and Manly Maladies**
> - Women were often seen as either **chaste** or **promiscuous** (see p.32). Once they'd had sex, women were thought to develop an **uncontrollable** appetite for **sex** and a tendency to become **hysterical**. **Hysteria** was considered to be a **feminine condition**. Ophelia's **madness** and bawdy songs in Act 4, Scene 5 have often been connected with **sexual hysteria** by critics such as Elaine Showalter (see p.68).
> - Hamlet's **melancholia** (depression) was a **fashionable condition** for **young men** at the time — it was thought to come from the part of the brain that produces **artistic** and **intellectual creativity** (see p.68).

2) However, Hamlet's **over-thinking** is also criticised for being **too feminine**. Claudius tells him that his **mourning** for his father is "**unmanly grief**" (1.2.94). A **popular idea** at the time was that **women talked** and **men acted** so Hamlet's **lack** of **action** combined with his long soliloquies make him see himself as **womanly** — "**Must like a whore unpack my heart with words**" (2.2.583).

...and Determines the way they Die

1) Even the way the characters **die** is **dictated** by their **gender**.

2) According to the conventions of **classical tragedy** (see p.54), men should **die** by the **sword** or in **combat** — Hamlet, Claudius, Polonius and Laertes are all **stabbed** or **cut** by **rapiers** (swords). Only King Hamlet dies in an **unmanly** way which emphasises that it was "**strange, and unnatural**" (1.5.28) and **not just because** he was **murdered** by his **own brother**.

3) In Elizabethan England, women's bodies were thought to be made of more '**watery**' substances than men. Their bodies were associated with **milk**, **blood** and **fluids** — so Gertrude **drinking** poison and Ophelia **drowning** are conventionally more '**feminine**' deaths.

4) When Laertes hears of Ophelia's death, he thinks that **crying** will get rid of his feminine side — his "**woman will be out**" (4.7.189).

John Everett Millais's painting 'Ophelia', shows Ophelia singing as she slips under the water.

© The Granger Collection/TopFoto

Gender and Sexuality

The Men in 'Hamlet' try to Restrict the Women's Sexuality

1) Hamlet thinks that his mother's **remarriage** to his uncle makes her a 'whore'. His **anger** at his **mother's sexuality** affects his view of all **women**. Hamlet uses **vulgar language** to make her sound like a **diseased prostitute**:

- He tells Horatio that Claudius has "**killed my King and whored my mother**" (5.2.64).
- He describes Gertrude's **sexual relationship** using **vivid imagery**. He says that she sleeps in "**the rank sweat of an enseamèd bed, / Stewed in corruption, honeying and making love / Over the nasty sty**" (3.4.93-95). The adjective "**enseamèd**" suggests a bed streaked in **animal grease** (or **semen**) and the word "**Stewed**" links to the word 'stew', the Elizabethan word for brothel.
- Hamlet may be influenced by the Ghost who **turns** his wife's sexuality into a **national crisis** in the "**royal bed of Denmark**" (1.5.82). Denmark is "**rotten**" (1.4.90), like the "**sty**" of Gertrude's bed.

2) The men in Ophelia's life assume that she's a **virgin** and use **language** that emphasises her bodily **purity**:

- Polonius and Laertes **lecture** Ophelia about the **dangers** of **young men** who might claim her "**chaste treasure**" (1.3.31) — having **sex** with her before she's **married**.
- Laertes grieves for her "**fair and unpolluted flesh**" (5.1.235) at her **graveside**.
- This language **enforces** Ophelia's **identity** as a **chaste maiden**, just as Hamlet does more **explicitly** when he orders "**Get thee to a nunnery**" (3.1.121) where she would have to be **celibate**.

3) The men use **abusive** and **accusatory** language in an attempt to **control** women's sexualities:

- Hamlet uses **suggestive language** when he asks Ophelia, "**Lady, shall I lie in your lap?**" (3.2.121). Ophelia says, "**I think nothing, my lord**" (3.2.126) because she's refusing to rise to the bait — if she acknowledged Hamlet's **sexual language**, it would suggest that she knows **more** than a maiden should.
- Using **military jargon**, Laertes makes a pun about men's **sexual advances** when he advises Ophelia to keep the "**rear of your affection, / Out of the shot and danger of desire**" (1.3.34-35). This is **designed** to embarrass Ophelia and make Laertes appear more **experienced** about **sexual** matters.

The play has an Underlying Concern with Incest

1) By **Elizabethan law** and according to **Christian beliefs**, Gertrude commits **incest** when she **marries** her **brother-in-law**. Hamlet calls Gertrude a "**husband's brother's wife**" (3.4.16) which emphasises this.
2) The Ghost accuses **Claudius** of being "**that incestuous, that adulterate beast**" (1.5.42) which **reinforces** Hamlet's **accusation** of incest and could imply that Claudius and Gertrude committed adultery while King Hamlet was **still alive** (see p.30).
3) Like Hamlet's **concerns** about his **mother's sexuality**, Laertes seems **obsessed** with his **sister's virginity** (see p.36).
4) Some directors have emphasised the potentially incestuous elements of the play, including Franco Zeffirelli who directed Hamlet and Gertrude in a **very sexual closet scene** (Act 3, Scene 4) in his 1990 film of *Hamlet*.

Practice Questions

Q1 Reread the Ghost's speech from Act 1, Scene 5 lines 34-91. What does the Ghost's language tell the audience about his feelings for Gertrude and her part in his murder? Pick out specific examples from the play.

Q2 Reread Laertes's and Polonius's advice to Ophelia in Act 1, Scene 3. How do these two characters present male sexuality to Ophelia and the audience?

Q3 Return to Ophelia's "madness" in Act 4, Scene 5, lines 17-74. How do Ophelia's songs and the reactions of the others in the court inform the audience about Ophelia's experiences in Elsinore?

"Why wouldst thou be a breeder of sinners?"

Elizabethans had some funny ideas about gender — but it was no joke being a woman in Elsinore. One false move and you were ruined. Or worse, pregnant out of marriage. A woman's life or body wasn't really her own, so this was the worst thing she could do.

Death

Death was everywhere in Elizabethan England — life expectancy was 40 years, infant mortality was high and disease was widespread. So compared with his love of stamp collecting, Hamlet's obsession with death is pretty understandable.

Hamlet's **Unsure** about what happens after **Death**

1) The **Reformation** brought new ideas about the **afterlife** to the newly-formed **Church of England**. However, many people still held on to **Catholic** ideas of the time about **spirits**, **demons** and **purgatory**.

2) In *Hamlet*, Shakespeare uses different **characters** to **introduce the conflict** between **Catholic**, **Protestant** and **humanist ideas**. The play **reflects** the **current debates** of Shakespeare's time:

- The Catholic Church **believes** in **purgatory**, a place where **souls** were **purified** of their **sins**. The Ghost may have **returned** to **earth** from purgatory but it's never specifically made **clear** (see p.40).

  > **Marcellus** voices the idea that **ghosts** were **visions** of their former **bodies**. These visions are made of "**the air**" so they can't be harmed, making them "**invulnerable**" (1.1.146).

- **Protestant** doctrine **rejected** the idea of **purgatory** — instead the dead went either to **heaven** or **hell**.

  > **Hamlet** calls **death** the "**undiscovered country**" (3.1.79). Once a person crosses over the "**bourn**" (boundary) of this country, "**No traveller returns**" (3.1.79-80).

  Without **purgatory**, there was also no reason to **pray** for the **souls** of the dead to make sure they went to **heaven**. Robert N. Watson argues that a revenger **addresses** the **balance** on **earth** and removes their own **guilt** by **avenging** their loved one's death instead of offering **prayers**.

- **Humanist** theories (see p.62) introduced a more **sceptical** view of spirits. Humanists such as **Reginald Scot** thought **ghosts** were the **product** of a **disturbed mind**, though they could also be **bad omens** of the **future**.

  > Like Hamlet, **Horatio** is a student at **Wittenberg**, and **educated** in **humanist** ideas. At first he tries to **dismiss** the Ghost, as a "**fantasy**" (1.1.23) and even directly addresses it as an "**illusion**" (1.1.128). After seeing it with his "**own eyes**" (1.1.58) he decides the Ghost is a "**prologue to the omen**" (1.1.123), or the **first sign** of **trouble**.

  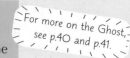
  For more on the Ghost, see p.40 and p.41.

Yorick's **Skull** is a **Reminder** of man's **Mortality**

Hans Holbein's painting 'The Ambassadors', completed in 1533.

1) In Elizabethan times, **death** was considered to be as much a part of **life** as **birth**. In *Hamlet,* Horatio refers to the "**womb of earth**" (1.1.138), which suggests that **burial** is a **return** to the **fertile soil** that supports **life** on earth.

> **Memento Mori**
>
> - Elizabethan **art** often used **images** of **skulls** as a **reminder** of **death** and man's **inescapable mortality**. This type of object is called a *memento mori*, which roughly translates as '**Remember, you will die**'.
> - Public **clocks**, statues, and **paintings** like Holbein's 'The Ambassadors' would be decorated with **skulls**. Holbein's painting has a **stretched** image of a **skull** (near the bottom edge). This **hidden** skull **reminds** the viewer that even when you **can't see** it, death is **near**.

2) Hamlet uses **Yorick's skull** as a **theatrical** *memento mori* in Act 5, Scene 1. Directors often decide to have Hamlet holding the skull up to his **face**, as if he's having a **conversation** with it. This represents Hamlet '**facing**' death out of **fascination** rather than **fear** or **bravery**. This is reflected in his language:

> Hamlet remembers Yorick's energy and "**infinite jest**" (5.1.182) as a court jester. Hamlet contrasts this **memory** with the **object** of the bare **skull** that Yorick's been **reduced** to. The thought of Yorick in such a state of decay makes him feel sick, "**My gorge rises at it**" (5.1.184-185), and he's moved by the thought that **everyone**, even kings, will be "**turned to clay**" (5.1.209).

Death

Suicide *was a* Sin *which* Barred *the* Soul's *entrance to* Heaven

1) **Suicide** was **condemned** by **Christian** teaching, and people who committed suicide were **buried** in **unconsecrated** (unblessed) ground. When the priest at Ophelia's funeral says that "**Shards, flints, and pebbles should be thrown on her**" (5.1.227) he's suggesting that she doesn't **deserve** a Christian funeral.

2) Hamlet is troubled by the **spiritual problems** of **suicide**. It's always on his mind — even when he's **joking**:

   - In Acts 1 and 2 Hamlet is **preoccupied** with the **thought** of suicide. Hamlet seems to want his **body** to **evaporate** — he asks for his "**flesh**" to "**melt**" and "**Thaw**" into "**dew**" (1.2.129-130). He doesn't **imagine** a **method** of "**self-slaughter**" (1.2.132) or refer to his own suicide — he talks about **oblivion** in an **abstract** way.

   - Hamlet jokes that when Polonius takes his **leave**, there's **nothing** that Polonius could "**take**" that would **please** Hamlet more "**except my life**" (2.2.215-217). Although Hamlet's making a pun on Polonius's words, his **repetition** of "**except my life, except my life**" makes it sound mournful, as if he's reciting a **prayer**.

3) Ophelia's **final words** on stage suggest that she **senses** that she's **going to die**:

   - In her final **song**, she sings "**Go to thy deathbed**" (4.5.193) — though the song is about an **old man**, it shows that she's got **death** on her mind. This is contrasted with the "**bride-bed**" (5.1.241) that Gertrude grieves for at Ophelia's **graveside**.

   - Ophelia's **final words** are "**God bye you**" (4.5.200) which is a contraction of '**God be with you**', the old way of saying '**goodbye**'. Ophelia says her **goodbyes** as she leaves the stage — it could suggest that she **knows** she's **not coming back**.

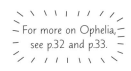
For more on Ophelia, see p.32 and p.33.

Death Restores Order *in Elsinore*

1) *Hamlet* **ends** with most of the main characters **dying**. The ambassador even returns to confirm that "**Rosencrantz and Guildenstern are dead**" (5.2.365). The **pile** of **bodies** is displayed "**High on a stage**" (5.2.372), which has a **double meaning**:

   - The bodies of Hamlet, Laertes, Claudius and Gertrude are to be **raised** onto a **platform** for display.

   - The **story** of their **deaths** should be shown on a **theatrical** stage. Horatio hopes to "**speak to th'yet unknowing world / How these things came about**" (5.2.373-374). Fortinbras agrees, asking for the "**noblest**" people to form the "**audience**" (5.2.381). These lines **emphasise** the play's own **theatricality**.

   > Horatio delivers what could be read as a '**prologue**' at the **end** of the play: "**So shall you hear / Of carnal, bloody, and unnatural acts**" (5.2.374-375). These lines suggest that the play we have just seen is the product of Horatio's promise to "**speak**". The play's **self-reflexive ending** makes it a new **beginning**.

2) The play shows how easily revenge can **spiral** out of **control** — **Hamlet** avenges **King Hamlet's** death, **Laertes** avenges **Polonius's** death and **Fortinbras** recovers his father's lost lands. Hamlet and Laertes's deaths **restore order** and close the revenge **cycle** neatly because there's **nobody left** to be **avenged**.

Practice Questions

Q1 "Let me not burst in ignorance. But tell / Why thy canonized bones, hearsèd in death, / Have burst their cerements" (1.4.46-48). How does Shakespeare present Hamlet's anxiety about the afterlife?

Q2 Imagine that Yorick's skull could speak. Write Yorick's answer to Hamlet's speech in Act 5, Scene 1, lines 181 to 212.

Q3 Suggest reasons why Shakespeare might have made Ophelia's death ambiguous? Refer to the text in your answer.

"'Tis common. All that lives must die"

What a bloody mess. Seriously, there's blood everywhere. Fortinbras must have thought he'd stumbled into a crazy party just as it was finishing... but instead of wine and party poppers all over the carpet, it's a bunch of dead royalty. Way to gate-crash, Fortinbras.

Appearance and Reality

It's hard for Hamlet to work out what's real and what's not in Elsinore. He tries to trust his own eyes, but anyone would start to doubt themselves if they saw the ghost of their own dead dad, trotting round the house at night in a full suit of armour...

In 'Hamlet' Appearances can be Deceptive

1) Hamlet **values truth**, and spends most of the play **searching** for it. In his search he's **continually frustrated** by the **inconsistencies** between **appearance** and **reality**.

2) To try to **understand** their **uncertain** reality, many of the characters in *Hamlet* want **visual proof** of things. Horatio has a **rational** approach to **truth**, saying "**I might not this believe / Without the sensible and true avouch / Of mine own eyes**" (1.1.56-58).

3) This **preoccupation** with **seeing** makes a **lack** of **sight** even more **disconcerting**:

> The play opens with **anxiety** caused by the **darkness**. When asked, "**is Horatio there?**", Horatio answers "**A piece of him**" (1.1.19). This suggests that there is so little **visibility** that Bernardo and Marcellus, who are employed to '**watch**' (in two senses — to **guard** and to **look out**) can only just make out his **hand**.

The Audience are Reminded that they're Watching a Play

1) **References** to the **stage** highlight the **blurred** line between **drama** and **life** and **appearance** and **reality**. Sometimes the audience are **separate observers**, and sometimes they're **addressed directly** as if the characters **know** they're there.

2) Hamlet uses **metaphorical language** to describe the **earth** and the **heavens** as a **theatre**. He even refers to the **Globe**, the **theatre** where Shakespeare's company performed (see p.52). The play is self-consciously theatrical and this **opens** the **space** of the **theatre** out into the **world**:

> - The line "**look you, this brave o'erhanging firmament, this majestical roof fretted with golden fire**" (2.2.300-301) may refer to the **roof** of the **Globe** which was **decorated** with **stars** and **planets**.
> - Hamlet says that "**memory holds a seat / In this distracted globe**" (1.5.96-97). This has a **triple reading** — of the "**globe**" as the **earth**, as a reference to the audience at the **Globe** theatre, or the "**globe**" as Hamlet's own **head**, full of distracted thoughts and memories.

3) These **reminders** mean that the audience is constantly aware that they're watching a **performance** — when a play, like *Hamlet*, draws attention to the fact that it's a **fictional** drama, it's called **metatheatre**.

The audience is Watching Hamlet Watch the King Watch a play

1) *Hamlet* is full of scenes where characters are **watching** or **spying** on each other. The fact that the **audience** is **watching** this from afar adds another **level** of **observation**.

2) This **complicates** the way the audience **watches** the play because they are caught up in a **network** of people **looking** at each other. Shakespeare's audience in the Globe would have been physically **close** to the stage, so the **separation** of the audience and the actors was **less obvious** than it is in modern theatres.

3) **Sight** is also described as a way to **control** or '**catch**' another person:

> - Hamlet hopes that he might be able to "**catch**" a **look** of **guilt** on Claudius's face when he watches *The Murder of Gonzago*: "**The play's the thing / Wherein I'll catch the conscience of the King**" (2.2.602-603).
> - When Claudius and Polonius **spy** on Ophelia and Hamlet's conversation in Act 3, Scene 1, they describe themselves as "**seeing unseen**" to "**gather**" (3.1.33-35) their **views** on Hamlet's behaviour.
> - Claudius asks Hamlet to "**remain / Here in the cheer and comfort of our eye**" (1.2.115-116). The **collective eye** of the **court** wants to **control** his **behaviour**, so it's unlikely it would be full of "**cheer**" or "**comfort**".

The Player King entertains Gertrude and Claudius (left) while Hamlet and Ophelia look on (bottom right)

© Alastair Muir/Rex Features

Appearance and Reality

Hamlet is Worried that Everyone's keeping up Fake Appearances

1) In Act 3 Hamlet presents Gertrude with the "**counterfeit presentment of two brothers**" (3.4.55). The word "**counterfeit**" means 'artificial copy' but was also a word for 'painting' during the Elizabethan era.

2) Throughout the play, several characters use the same metaphor of **painting** (especially related to **duplicity**, see p.12) to **emphasise** a more general **fear** that **reality** can be **masked** by a superficial **image**:

   - Hamlet **attacks** women's **vanity**: "**I have heard of your paintings too, well enough. God hath given you one face, and you make yourselves another**" (3.1.143-145). He links the use of **cosmetics** to a **betrayal** of God's **intentions**.

   - He **warns** that no matter how people **change** their **appearances** in **life**, **death** will claim **everyone** anyway: "**let her paint an inch thick, to this favour she must come**" (5.1.190-191).

   - Claudius draws a **parallel** between "**The harlot's cheek, beautied with plastering art**" and his **secret crimes** — "**my deed to my most painted word**" (3.1.51-53). This comparison suggests that Claudius's **impressive** language, which he uses to **cover up** the reality of his **shameful** actions, is similar to how **prostitutes** used make-up to **cover** a **face** possibly **scarred** by **syphilis**.

Hamlet doesn't Know Who to Trust

1) Hamlet believes that he's **more perceptive** than those around him because he's searching for the **truth**. Hamlet thinks **everyone else** is **happy** to **accept** the **deception** around them and therefore **can't** be **trusted**.

2) However, the **sight** of the **Ghost** raises **problematic questions** about Hamlet's **perception**:

   - The **visibility** of the Ghost seems to be **universal** at first — Marcellus, Bernardo, Horatio and Hamlet all "**approve our eyes and speak to it**" (1.1.29). This seems to be enough to **prove** that the Ghost is **real**.

   - However, in Gertrude's **bedroom** in Act 3, Scene 4, Hamlet appears to "**bend**" his **sight** on what Gertrude sees as "**vacancy**" (3.4.118). This makes **Gertrude** think that Hamlet must be **mad**.

     > Gertrude refers to "**th'incorporal air**" (3.4.119) and "**bodiless... ecstasy**" (3.4.139). She uses a **tautology** (**repeating** words with the **same meaning**) to **reinforce** her **message**: air is always 'incorporal' and 'ecstasy' comes from the Greek word for 'outside the body' so it already means "**bodiless**". Gertrude's **repetitive** language **emphasises** the fact that Hamlet's vision seems **impossible** to her.

   - Hamlet's **frustrated** that the Ghost **seems** to be **selectively** visible to him this time, and demands "**look you there**" (3.4.135), but he can't **control** Gertrude's sight, and he can't **prove** what he has seen.

3) These encounters leave the audience **uncertain** about what they have seen. The Ghost might be "**the very coinage of [Hamlet's] brain**" (3.4.138) or it might be that Hamlet's "**prophetic soul**" (1.5.40) sees **truth** where others don't.

4) Hamlet's **search** for the **truth** is made **more difficult** because those around him are being so **deceptive**. Claudius's **letter** to **kill Hamlet**, the **cup** of **poison** and the **poisoned swords**, Polonius's **eavesdropping** and Ophelia's **willingness** to be used in the **plans** to **spy** on Hamlet all **contribute** to the levels of deception in the court.

Practice Questions

Q1 How would you stage the first scene of Act 1 in order to emphasise the poor visibility? Think about the set, lighting and sound effects and use quotations from the play to explain your decisions.

Q2 "'Seems', madam? Nay, it is. I know not 'seems'". How does Hamlet make the distinction between his inward emotions and his outward display of them? Refer to the text in your answer.

Q3 What hidden information might the audience of *Hamlet* deduce about the characters while they watch *The Mousetrap*?

"For by the image of my cause I see / The portraiture of his"

Secrets, false identities, spies and lies abound. What makes it more unsettling is that the audience seem to see more than Hamlet himself, but there's so much that isn't clear, so no one can be certain of the truth. Which is a relief for you, starting out on an essay.

Performing 'Hamlet'

'Hamlet' is a play that's fascinated audiences for over 400 years. Quite a claim to fame. There must be something about it that keeps us coming back for more. Maybe it's all the raunchy sex scenes. Oh wait, there aren't any. Must be something else...

Shakespeare was *Influenced* by *Older* versions of the *'Hamlet'* story

1) Some scholars think that a **different version** of the *Hamlet* story was performed from **1589** onwards. This earlier version **isn't well recorded** and is referred to as the ***Ur-Hamlet*** (before-Hamlet). It's thought that Thomas Kyd, the author of *The Spanish Tragedy,* may be responsible for producing the *Ur-Hamlet*.

2) However, other scholars think that **Shakespeare** developed the character of Hamlet over **several years**. Even the **scripts** of *Hamlet* still in **existence** today have big **differences** between them so there is evidence that Shakespeare was **redrafting** the play as it was performed.

3) Shakespeare may also have been **influenced** by **older** texts:

   - One of these was the legend of **Amleth**, a tale about the son of a **Danish** king **murdered** by his **brother**, written in the 13th century. This legend has many similarities with Shakespeare's *Hamlet*, including Amleth's **feigned madness** and his **exile** to Britain, the second **marriage** of the **queen**, Gerutha (which sounds a bit like Gertrude) and the **death** of a **spy** (like Polonius's death in *Hamlet*).

   - There's evidence to suggest that Shakespeare had read **Timothy Bright's** *A Treatise of Melancholy*, published in **1586**. This was a **popular** and **influential** book on '**melancholia**'. Critics such as John Dover Wilson argue that Hamlet shows all the **symptoms** Bright describes: "**melancholick humour [brings] terrible objects to the fantasie**". Horatio similarly says that the **Ghost's "horrible form"** draws Hamlet "**into madness**" (1.5.72-74).

Shakespeare's plays were *Performed* at the *Globe Theatre*

1) There was an increase in theatre **building** at the end of the **16th century**.

2) **The Lord Chamberlain's Men**, Shakespeare's acting **company**, built the **Globe** in 1599. Archaeologists think that it was a **round**, **three-storey** building with an **open-air** central '**pit**' where the audience could **stand** to watch the plays.

3) More **expensive** seats would be in the **covered** areas around the **outside** of the building, looking down on the **stage** jutting out into the **pit**.

The Globe, rebuilt in 1997, on the site of the original theatre on the bank of the River Thames.

> **The Globe's Reconstruction**
>
> The Globe was burnt down by a misfired **cannon** during a performance of *Henry VIII* in **1613**. It was **rebuilt**, and then **demolished** again during a **ban** of **theatres** in the **1640s**. A new **Globe Theatre** was rebuilt at the old site in **1997**.

Elizabethan Theatres were *Different* from *Today's Theatres*

1) Shakespeare called the Globe a "**wooden O**" in *Henry V* — the **round** walls and empty '**pit**' make it an **unusual** theatre compared to the modern convention to clearly **separate** the audience and stage.

> **Elizabethan Theatre Structure**
>
> - There was **less distinction** between **audience** and **actors** because the **stage** was positioned **among the audience**. Instead of an arch, there was a **roof** across the **back half** of the stage, which was **painted** with **clouds** and **stars** to look like the '**heavens**'.
>
> - The stage had no **wings** to **hide props** or **extra characters** and **no curtain** to drop at the **interval** or **scene changes**. Anything that happened **on stage** had to be **part of the performance**. Characters that **died** on stage had to be **carried** off by **other characters**, e.g. Hamlet removes **Polonius's body**: "**I'll lug the guts into the neighbour room**" (3.4.213).

2) The Elizabethan theatre **wasn't concerned** with looking '**realistic**'. It might seem **odd** to **modern audiences** that all of Shakespeare's plays were performed by a **male-only cast** (as women weren't allowed on stage during Elizabethan times), but the Elizabethan theatre was more about **gesture** and **symbolism** than being '**true**' to life.

Performing 'Hamlet'

'Hamlet' has been *Staged* in *Different* ways since Shakespeare's time

1) *Hamlet* is traditionally a popular play to perform. Directors of **modern productions** of *Hamlet* face **challenges** about how to **stage** and **adapt** the play for **today's audiences**.

2) Some companies perform the play **in full** and in **Elizabethan costume**. Others **cut scenes** and **change** the **setting** or **locations**, sometimes to **react** to **political** or **social concerns** at the time of the performance.

- In **1980**, **Richard Eyre** directed a version of *Hamlet* with **no Ghost**. The first scene, where Marcellus, Bernardo and Horatio **see** the Ghost, was **cut** — instead **Hamlet** spoke the **Ghost's lines** as if he was **possessed** by the **spirit** of his dead father. This decision **shifts** the **problem** of the Ghost's presence as a **contradiction** to **Protestant ideas** to **uncertainty** over Hamlet's **madness**.
- In **1988**, **Derek Jacobi** directed a **version** of *Hamlet* where the **final line** of the play, "**Go, bid the soldiers shoot**" (5.2.397) was **interpreted** as an instruction from Fortinbras to his **soldiers** to **shoot** the **remaining** members of Claudius's court, including **Horatio**.
- **Janet Suzman's 2006 version** of *Hamlet* juxtaposed a **traditional performance** of the play with **South Africa's political context**. The director kept the full script and Elizabethan language but used **modern military costumes** and a **multi-racial cast**. This could be used to represent the **stresses** of **apartheid** and **violence** in Cape Town.

Hamlet's also made *Appearances* on the *Big Screen*

1) Transferring *Hamlet* from the **empty stage** of the **Globe** to the **cinema** can raise difficulties. The standard **shorter length** of **films** mean that directors often decide to **cut** certain scenes, or **focus** on **different aspects** of the play.

- In **Laurence Olivier's 1948** adaptation of *Hamlet*, the more **political** scenes with Fortinbras were **removed** in order to **emphasise** the **intense family relationships**.
- **Franco Zeffirelli** also focused on the families in his 1990 film production. Zeffirelli directed **Mel Gibson** and **Glenn Close** as Hamlet and Gertrude in a **highly sexualised** version of the **bedroom scene** in Act 3, Scene 4.

2) Other film directors have decided to **change** the **setting** in order to **comment** on the **play** itself or to **use** the play as a **commentary** on **current issues**.

- **Kenneth Branagh's full-length** film version of *Hamlet* (1996) is set in the **19th century**, using **Blenheim Palace** in England as the setting for the court of Elsinore. Branagh's adaptation shows **sex scenes** involving **Hamlet** and **Ophelia**, removing the **ambiguity** surrounding Ophelia's **virginity**.
- **Michael Almereyda** adapted *Hamlet* in **2000** in a **modern day** version set in **Manhattan**. The **Ghost** is spotted on **CCTV** and **Denmark** is the name of a **business**, not a country, reflecting **current concerns** about **capitalism** and **corruption** in big business.

Practice Questions

Q1 How would the Globe's audiences' experience of *Hamlet* be different from that of a cinema-goer in the 20th century?

Q2 Reread the final scene of the play. How would you stage this scene in the traditional 'round' at the Globe Theatre?

Q3 Does *Hamlet* belong to Shakespeare's time, or is it something directors should update and adapt? Explain your answer with examples from productions you have seen or read about.

"Let this same be presently performed, / Even while men's minds are wild"

From a boat to a box set, productions of 'Hamlet' have been seen in the most unlikely of places. It's always a good plan to see a stage or film production before you finish the course, or you could always get some friends together and do a D.I.Y. 'Hamlet'...

Form and Structure

'Hamlet' is a tragedy... but it's not just because it's a tragic story. If only it were that simple. It's also because it fulfils certain tragic characteristics laid out by Aristotle, an Ancient Greek philosopher. I personally prefer Asterix.

Aristotle **Influenced** what people thought about **Tragedies**

1) Tragedy dates back to the **sixth century BC** in **Ancient Greece**. The Greek tragedies have mostly been **lost**, but they were **imitated** by the **Roman** playwright, **Seneca** (see p.42). **Shakespeare** was **familiar** with **Seneca's** plays.

2) In the **fourth century BC**, the philosopher **Aristotle** wrote down the **rules** for **Greek tragedy** in his *Poetics*.

3) Although **Shakespeare** may not have read it, Aristotle's **theory** was used by **neoclassicists** to analyse *Hamlet* (see p.64).

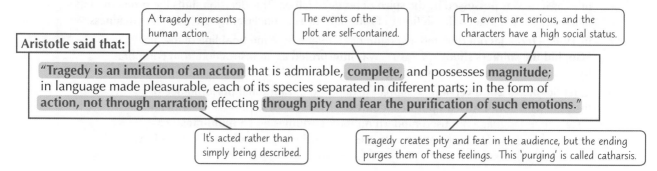

Aristotle said that:

A tragedy represents human action.

The events of the plot are self-contained.

The events are serious, and the characters have a high social status.

"**Tragedy is an imitation of an action** that is admirable, **complete**, and possesses **magnitude**; in language made pleasurable, each of its species separated in different parts; in the form of **action, not through narration**; effecting **through pity and fear the purification of such emotions**."

It's acted rather than simply being described.

Tragedy creates pity and fear in the audience, but the ending purges them of these feelings. This 'purging' is called catharsis.

3) Aristotle thought that there were **six main parts** to a **tragedy** which he **ranked** in order of **importance**:

1) **Plot** (structure of events)
2) **Character**
3) **Thought** (the play's values and characters' thoughts)

4) **Diction** (use of language)
5) **Lyric Poetry** (or **Song**)
6) **Spectacle** (how the play looks and sounds)

4) For Aristotle, **plot** is "**the most important thing of all**", while the **characters only** exist to **develop** the plot. According to Aristotle, the plot should have a **strict tragic structure**:

- **Unity** — The play should be **self-contained** — **every event** should **contribute** to the **plot**.
- **Protagonist** — He should be a fairly **noble** character who is **virtuous, powerful** and **brave**.
- **Mistake** — The protagonist should make a **mistake** which leads to a **reversal** in fortune (a **sudden change** that leads to the protagonist's **downfall**). The Greek word Aristotle uses for 'mistake' has **several interpretations**. It could mean a 'sin', 'error', 'misunderstanding' or 'tragic flaw'.
- **Realisation** — The hero **realises** their **mistake** and becomes **aware** of how they have **destroyed themselves**.
- **Catharsis** — The **audience's pity** and **fear** at the play's **climax** should lead to an **emotional release**.

Aristotle's ideas about **Tragic Form** can be applied to 'Hamlet'

Although Shakespeare may not have directly read Aristotle's work, he was influenced by other **Elizabethan** playwrights who did, like Ben Jonson. Neoclassical critics also used Aristotle's *Poetics* as a way of looking at tragic drama, so it's useful to see how *Hamlet* might fit into Aristotle's **tragic structure**:

UNITY — *Hamlet* is a **complete** play and most of the events **lead on** from **one another**. However, the pirates episode in Act 4, Scene 6 is a '**deus ex machina**' — it's an **unrealistic plot device** which doesn't seem to **fit in** with the rest of the play.

For more about the pirates scene, see p.20.

PROTAGONIST — Hamlet is of **noble birth** and is described as "**sweet and commendable**" (1.2.87) which suggests he's a **virtuous hero**. However, he is also morally a bit **ambiguous**.

MISTAKE — Hamlet's **death** could be **caused** by his **tragic flaw** of being **unable to act** or alternatively, it could be the result of **mistakenly killing** Polonius — it depends how you **interpret** Aristotle's **use** of the word '**mistake**'.

REALISATION — This could perhaps occur in **Act 5, Scene 1**, when Hamlet **returns** from **England** (see p.23).

CATHARSIS — The end of the play, including Hamlet's death, purges the audience of their **pity** and **fear**. Claudius's death puts an end to the **corruption** of the court and Fortinbras helps to restore **order** in Denmark.

Form and Structure

'Hamlet' is set in just One Place — Elsinore Castle

1) By setting his tragedy around **one place**, Shakespeare **reduced** the **number** of **scene changes**. Also, if *Hamlet* is staged in a **single location**, it **intensifies** the drama:

- As the "**rotten**" (1.4.90) **court** represents the **state**, the **castle** becomes a **microcosm** of **Denmark**. For Hamlet, the **castle** is a **claustrophobic cell** in the "**prison**" (2.2.243) of Denmark.

- The distinction between **public** and **private spaces** becomes **blurred**. There seems to be nowhere to hide as **spies** are everywhere. Even Gertrude's **closet** is **open** to the **audience's view** in Act 3, Scene 4.

- Several references are made to the **sea** or to "**the dreadful summit of the cliff**" (1.4.70), which has led many directors and critics to imagine Elsinore to be on a **cliff edge**. This emphasises Elsinore's **isolation** and Hamlet's **restricted** life.

Franco Zeffirelli used Dunnottar Castle in Scotland as the location for Elsinore in his 1990 film version of Hamlet (see p.53)

© Patrick Frilet/Rex Features

2) While the play focuses on the **court**, several **journeys** take place **offstage**. Hamlet leaves to travel to **England**, Laertes visits **Paris**, Horatio has returned from **Wittenberg**, Ophelia dies in a **river** near the castle grounds and Rosencrantz and Guildenstern die in **England**. These are **suggestions** of **places** beyond Elsinore but, as the audience **don't see them**, they only **increase** the **sense** of **isolation** and **claustrophobia** on stage.

Hamlet Loses his Sense of Time throughout the play

1) At the **beginning** of the play, **time** moves quite **slowly** and at a **regular pace**. The audience is given **details** of **dates** and **times** of events, e.g. King Hamlet is "**two months dead**" (1.2.138) and Claudius was married to Gertrude "**within a month**" (1.2.145).

2) However, by Act 3, Hamlet has **lost** his **purpose** as a **revenger** and along with this, his **sense** of **time**. He tells Ophelia that his "**father died within's two hours**" (3.2.136). The play's time progression becomes **disorientating** and **irregular**, making Hamlet's behaviour seem more **erratic**.

3) At the start of the play, **day** and **night** are used to **divide public courtly life** and the **hidden underworld** of the **Ghost's appearances**. However, the division **breaks down** later in the play when it becomes **less clear** what **time** of **day** it is, or **how many** days have passed **between scenes**.

- Hamlet repeatedly says "**Good night**" (3.4.218) at the end of the **closet scene** in Act 3, Scene 4. These lines suggest that it's night time and Hamlet's "**good night**" is followed by Claudius's line "**The sun no sooner shall the mountains touch**" (4.1.29) which **confirms** the time of day at the beginning of Act 4.

- By Act 4, Scene 5, Ophelia is singing "**Good night, ladies, good night**" (4.5.73). However, Ophelia's **madness** and the **multiple scene changes** mean that the audience **aren't sure** what night it is or whether it is **night at all**.

Practice Questions

Q1 How does Hamlet's 'error in judgement' lead to his own downfall?

Q2 Write out a plot summary for an adaptation of *Hamlet*, in which Hamlet doesn't kill Polonius.

Q3 How does Shakespeare use time and space to emphasise Hamlet's emotional journey as a revenger?

"I could be bounded in a nutshell"

Shakespeare has his own ideas about structure. He sets everything in one court, but sends characters outside. He starts the play off like clockwork and ends it in hurried confusion. His tragic hero doesn't want the job of being a tragic hero. Shake it up Shakesy.

Dramatic Language

If someone goes to the effort of organising everything they say into rhythmic, ten syllable rhyming lines there's usually a reason.
They're either rapping into a hairbrush in the bathroom mirror, or they're delivering an important speech in a Shakespeare play.

Shakespeare uses Blank Verse to imitate the rhythm of Natural Speech

1) The **rhythm** of English speech **naturally** follows a **pattern** of emphasising **every other syllable**.

2) This rhythm is called **iambic**. An **iamb** is a **measurement** of **two syllables** that goes 'duh-**dum**'.
   A string of **five iambs** makes **ten syllables** of alternating stress — this is called **iambic pentameter**:

   >   1 **2**   3   **4**   5 **6**   7   **8**   9 **10**
   > "For **in** that **sleep** of **death** what **dreams** may **come**" (3.1.66).
   > (duh-**dum**) (duh-**dum**) (duh-**dum**) (duh-**dum**)   (duh - **dum**)

3) In the sixteenth century, poets started to write in **unrhymed** iambic pentameter — this is **blank verse**.

4) Shakespeare uses the **10-syllable framework** of blank verse to imitate
   formal speech — lines that are written in **blank verse** are usually spoken by **high
   status** characters (e.g. Hamlet) or form part of a **speech** or **soliloquy**.

5) Some **crucial moments** in Hamlet's speeches are marked by **changing** the pattern
   of iambic pentameter — Hamlet's soliloquy in Act 3, Scene 1 is **interrupted**
   by a **caesura** (break) which breaks the **rhythm** of the **iambic metre**. There's also
   an **extra syllable** in the line which suggests Hamlet is **thinking on his feet**.

© Alastair Muir/Rex Features

   >   caesura
   > 1 **2**   3 **4**   5 **6**   7 8   9 **10** 11
   > "To **be**, or **not**   to **be** — **that** is   the **quest**ion" (3.1.56)
   > (duh-**dum**)(duh-**dum**)(duh-**dum**) (**dum**-duh) (duh-**dum**) (duh-)

Sometimes the verse Breaks Down into Prose

1) Prose is writing that's **not verse** — it **doesn't rhyme**, it's got **no metre** and there are **no line breaks**.

2) When characters **talk** to each other **informally** or address a character of a **lower social status**, they use **prose**.

   > The **lack** of **ceremony** displayed in Act 5, Scene 1 by the Gravedigger, Hamlet and Horatio
   > when they joke about death is **reflected** in their use of **prose**. This **informality** is **juxtaposed**
   > with the **return** to **blank verse** when Ophelia's funeral procession arrives. The **transition** from
   > prose to verse is marked by a rare example of **rhyming iambic pentameter** (5.1.209-212).

3) At other points, the characters' **control** over their **language slips** which reflects their state of **mind**. Prose can be
   used to show that a character can't **organise** their **thoughts** in **eloquent iambic pentameter**. When Ophelia goes
   mad in Act 4, Scene 5, she speaks to the court in **prose**, which reflects her **rambling** and **incoherent** thoughts.

Shakespeare uses Rhetoric to give his Language more Power

1) Shakespeare's language is full of **tricks** and **flourishes** that make his writing more **powerful**.
   These **techniques** are part of a **general practice** of making **speeches persuasive** called 'rhetoric'.

2) Shakespeare often uses these **rhetorical devices** (see glossary for more):

Repetition	**Alliteration** (placing words that begin with the same sound near each other) and **anaphora** (starting phrases or sentences with the same word).	"Marry, this is miching mallecho. It means mischief." (3.2.146).
Puns	**Homophones** are different words that sound the same and **homographs** are words that have the same spelling.	The homophone in the line "that the Everlasting had not fixed / His **canon** 'gainst self-slaughter" (1.2.131-132) connects church law (canon) with the military weapon (cannon).
Exaggeration	Use of **hyperbole** (stretching the point for emphasis) and **superlatives** (saying something is the "most" or "least").	Claudius uses a superlative to blame Hamlet for being the "**most** violent author / Of his own just remove" (4.5.81-82).

Dramatic Language

Hamlet has many Soliloquies — each with a Different Purpose

1) In *Hamlet*, characters sometimes **express** their **thoughts** to each other but often just to **themselves**.

- **Short outbursts** or **comments** directed at the **audience** are called **asides**, e.g. Hamlet's first line in the play **"A little more than kin, and less than kind"** (1.2.65) might be considered an aside because Claudius **doesn't** seem to **notice** it and carries on with his question. This **witty aside** introduces Hamlet as an **intelligent outsider**, who comments **privately** on the events for the **audience's benefit**.

- A **long speech** delivered to **other characters** on stage is called a **monologue**, e.g. Laertes's lecture to Ophelia (1.3.10-44). The speaker is talking **directly** to those present **without** much **interruption**.

- A **long speech** performed in **private**, or while the character **thinks** they are **alone**, is called a **soliloquy**. Soliloquies are **introspective reflections** that **communicate** the character's **inner thoughts** to the **audience**. Soliloquies are especially important in *Hamlet* and may reflect the **humanist** interest in the self (see p.42).

2) Hamlet has **five** major soliloquies in the play — each gives the audience some **insight** into his **struggle** with his **role** as a **revenger**, and reveals a **different** side to his character. It's **useful** to **study** each of them **closely** to get a **better understanding** of Hamlet's **complex** character.

If you're not sure what any of these words mean, check the glossary on p.78-79.

"O that this too too sullied flesh would melt" (1.2.129-159)

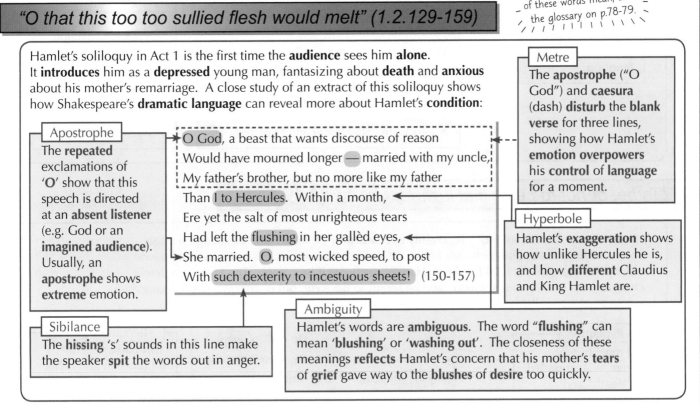

Hamlet's soliloquy in Act 1 is the first time the **audience** sees him **alone**. It **introduces** him as a **depressed** young man, fantasizing about **death** and **anxious** about his mother's remarriage. A close study of an extract of this soliloquy shows how Shakespeare's **dramatic language** can reveal more about Hamlet's **condition**:

Metre

The **apostrophe** ("O God") and **caesura** (dash) **disturb** the **blank verse** for three lines, showing how Hamlet's **emotion overpowers** his **control** of **language** for a moment.

Apostrophe

The **repeated** exclamations of 'O' show that this speech is directed at an **absent listener** (e.g. God or an **imagined audience**). Usually, an **apostrophe** shows **extreme** emotion.

> O God, a beast that wants discourse of reason
> Would have mourned longer — married with my uncle,
> My father's brother, but no more like my father
> Than I to Hercules. Within a month,
> Ere yet the salt of most unrighteous tears
> Had left the flushing in her gallèd eyes,
> She married. O, most wicked speed, to post
> With such dexterity to incestuous sheets! (150-157)

Hyperbole

Hamlet's **exaggeration** shows how unlike Hercules he is, and how **different** Claudius and King Hamlet are.

Sibilance

The **hissing** 's' sounds in this line make the speaker **spit** the words out in anger.

Ambiguity

Hamlet's words are **ambiguous**. The word **"flushing"** can mean '**blushing**' or '**washing out**'. The closeness of these meanings **reflects** Hamlet's concern that his mother's **tears** of **grief** gave way to the **blushes** of **desire** too quickly.

Practice Questions

Q1 Reread the beginning of Act 1, Scene 2, from lines 1 to 39. Discuss the effect of blank verse in Claudius's speech.

Q2 Discuss the importance of asides and soliloquies in relation to the play's audience.

Q3 Rewrite Hamlet's soliloquy in Act 1, Scene 2 in your own words.

"Words, words, words"

To write in verse of ten syll'bles is hard / And as dear Will, our Shakey knows, it's tough / T'Attempt to write in feet of equal stress. / As if soliloquies weren't hard enough / If I had to rhyme I'd just end a mess / Whereas Shakespeare wrote blank verse by the yard.

Dramatic Language

Hamlet's soliloquies are jam-packed with dramatic techniques and rhetorical flourishes — Shakespeare's really thrown his best stuff at them. To give you a bit of a hand, here are some examples of close reading and literary terms to get your head around.

"O, what a rogue and peasant slave am I!" (2.2.547-603)

Hamlet's longest soliloquy occurs just after he talks to the players. Hamlet's **frustration** is shown in the language of this soliloquy — his swearing "**Fie upon't, foh!**" (2.2.585), questions "**Am I a coward?**" (2.2.568) and apostrophe "**O, vengeance!**" (2.2.579) **interrupt** the **rhythm** of the **blank verse**. He wrestles with his **guilt** until he **makes** a plan to "**catch the conscience of the King**" (2.2.603). The soliloquy ends with a **rhyming couplet** — the **neatness** of this ending creates a sense that Hamlet is **confident** and back in **control**.

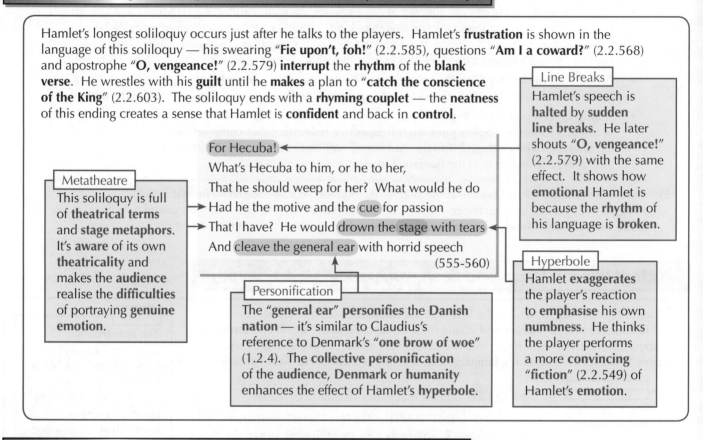

Line Breaks

Hamlet's speech is **halted** by **sudden line breaks**. He later shouts "**O, vengeance!**" (2.2.579) with the same effect. It shows how **emotional** Hamlet is because the **rhythm** of his language is **broken**.

Metatheatre

This soliloquy is full of **theatrical terms** and **stage metaphors**. It's **aware** of its own **theatricality** and makes the **audience** realise the **difficulties** of portraying **genuine emotion**.

For Hecuba!
What's Hecuba to him, or he to her,
That he should weep for her? What would he do
Had he the motive and the cue for passion
That I have? He would drown the stage with tears
And cleave the general ear with horrid speech
(555-560)

Personification

The "**general ear**" personifies the **Danish nation** — it's similar to Claudius's reference to Denmark's "**one brow of woe**" (1.2.4). The **collective personification** of the **audience**, **Denmark** or **humanity** enhances the effect of Hamlet's **hyperbole**.

Hyperbole

Hamlet **exaggerates** the player's reaction to **emphasise** his own **numbness**. He thinks the player performs a more **convincing** "**fiction**" (2.2.549) of Hamlet's **emotion**.

"To be, or not to be — that is the question" (3.1.56-89)

Hamlet's most **famous** soliloquy is possibly **overheard** by Ophelia, who's reading on stage, and Claudius and Polonius, who are hiding off stage. However, as he's **not aware** of anyone else's presence until the final two lines, Hamlet speaks **as if** he's **alone**. The **tone** completely **changes** from his previous soliloquy and he seems to have **run out** of **energy**. His lines regularly run on to **eleven syllables**, which suggests he's **trailing off** at the **ends** of his **lines**.

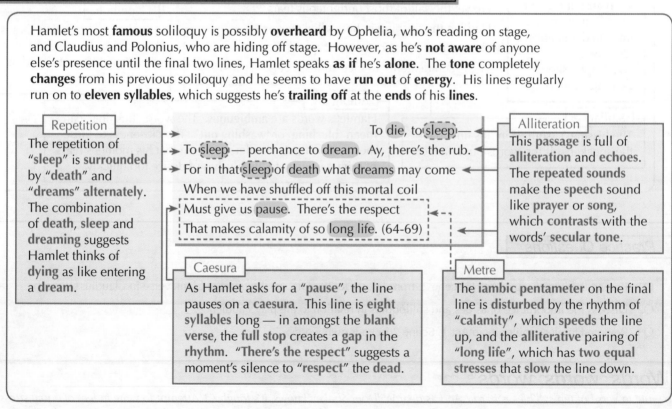

Repetition

The repetition of "sleep" is **surrounded** by "death" and "dreams" alternately. The combination of **death, sleep** and **dreaming** suggests Hamlet thinks of **dying** as like entering a **dream**.

Alliteration

This **passage** is full of **alliteration** and **echoes**. The **repeated sounds** make the **speech** sound like **prayer** or **song**, which **contrasts** with the words' **secular tone**.

To die, to sleep —
To sleep — perchance to dream. Ay, there's the rub.
For in that sleep of death what dreams may come
When we have shuffled off this mortal coil
Must give us pause. There's the respect
That makes calamity of so long life. (64-69)

Caesura

As Hamlet asks for a "**pause**", the line pauses on a **caesura**. This line is **eight syllables** long — in amongst the **blank verse**, the **full stop** creates a **gap** in the **rhythm**. "**There's the respect**" suggests a moment's silence to "**respect**" the **dead**.

Metre

The **iambic pentameter** on the final line is **disturbed** by the rhythm of "**calamity**", which **speeds** the line up, and the **alliterative** pairing of "**long life**", which has **two equal stresses** that **slow** the line down.

Dramatic Language

"Now might I do it pat, now 'a is a-praying" (3.3.73-96)

After Claudius delivers his **only soliloquy** in the play, Hamlet's **tone** returns to the **frustrated call** for **action** found in his soliloquy in Act 2, Scene 2. However, his use of **financial language** suggests he's prepared to **bargain**.

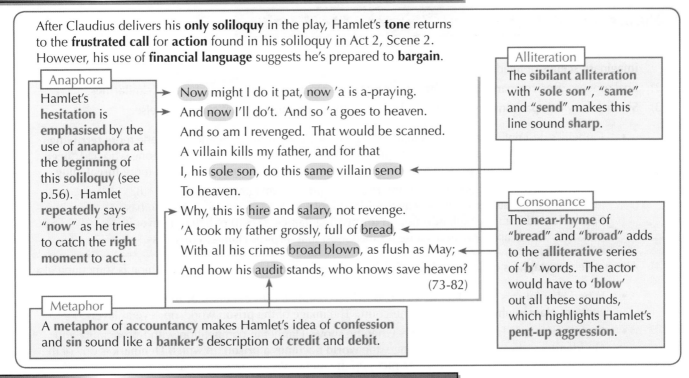

Anaphora

Hamlet's **hesitation** is **emphasised** by the use of **anaphora** at the **beginning** of this **soliloquy** (see p.56). Hamlet **repeatedly** says "**now**" as he tries to catch the **right moment** to act.

Now might I do it pat, now 'a is a-praying.
And now I'll do't. And so 'a goes to heaven.
And so am I revenged. That would be scanned.
A villain kills my father, and for that
I, his sole son, do this same villain send
To heaven.
Why, this is hire and salary, not revenge.
'A took my father grossly, full of bread,
With all his crimes broad blown, as flush as May;
And how his audit stands, who knows save heaven?
(73-82)

Alliteration

The **sibilant alliteration** with "**sole son**", "**same**" and "**send**" makes this line sound **sharp**.

Consonance

The **near-rhyme** of "**bread**" and "**broad**" adds to the **alliterative** series of 'b' words. The actor would have to 'blow' out all these sounds, which highlights Hamlet's **pent-up aggression**.

Metaphor

A **metaphor** of **accountancy** makes Hamlet's idea of **confession** and **sin** sound like a **banker's** description of **credit** and **debit**.

"How all occasions do inform against me" (4.4.32-66)

Hamlet's **last soliloquy** shows him again trying to be a **revenger**. By **comparing** himself with **Fortinbras** and a "**beast**" (4.4.35) he sets himself an **ultimatum** that he must **act** or be **reduced** to just his worthless **thoughts**.

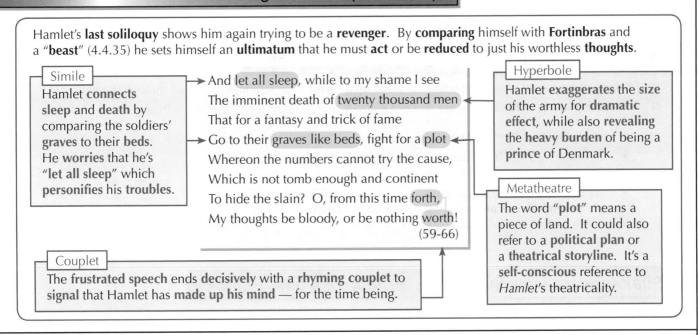

Simile

Hamlet **connects** **sleep** and **death** by comparing the soldiers' **graves** to their **beds**. He **worries** that he's "**let all sleep**" which **personifies** his **troubles**.

And let all sleep, while to my shame I see
The imminent death of twenty thousand men
That for a fantasy and trick of fame
Go to their graves like beds, fight for a plot
Whereon the numbers cannot try the cause,
Which is not tomb enough and continent
To hide the slain? O, from this time forth,
My thoughts be bloody, or be nothing worth!
(59-66)

Hyperbole

Hamlet **exaggerates** the **size** of the army for **dramatic effect**, while also **revealing** the **heavy burden** of being a **prince** of Denmark.

Metatheatre

The word "**plot**" means a piece of land. It could also refer to a **political plan** or a **theatrical storyline**. It's a **self-conscious** reference to *Hamlet*'s theatricality.

Couplet

The **frustrated speech** ends **decisively** with a **rhyming couplet** to **signal** that Hamlet has **made up his mind** — for the time being.

Practice Questions

Q1 Discuss the effect and use of the caesura in Hamlet's soliloquies.

Q2 How do Hamlet's soliloquies affect the audience's understanding of his character?

Q3 How might Hamlet have changed his soliloquy in Act 3, Scene 1 had he known he was being listened to?

"Thus conscience does make cowards of us all"

Blimey. Hamlet's soliloquies are dense and difficult things to read. And what makes it worse is Hamlet's uncertainty — his strength and resolve makes way for nervous meditation, only to be overridden by a surge in confidence again. Make your mind up Ham!

Imagery

"If hairs be wires, black wires grow on her head." Oh, that's nice, Will. Shakespeare's imagery is not always as naff as it is in Sonnet 130. In 'Hamlet', for instance, Shakespeare uses it as a tool that helps him to fire up the audience's imagination.

Simile and Metaphor create Images out of Words

1) Shakespeare uses **figurative language** that appeals to the **senses**. He uses language to conjure up **imaginary scenes** or to add **further meaning**. This type of technique is broadly called '**imagery**'.

2) Shakespeare uses **comparisons** to **connect separate images** or **ideas** and suggest shared **similarities**.

3) **Similes** draw **comparisons** between things by saying that something is '**like**' something else:

- Ophelia's description of Hamlet's **mad acting** in her closet in Act 2, Scene 1 is made more **terrifying** by the simile that **compares** Hamlet's "**piteous**" look with the appearance of someone who had "**been loosèd out of hell / To speak of horrors**" (2.1.82-84). It makes his **madness** seem more **threatening**.
- The **simile** gives the audience a startling **reference point** to **imagine** his "**look**" (2.1.82). It also **reminds** the **audience** of the way the **Ghost looks** in Act 1, Scene 5 — as if he has been **released** from the "**sulphurous and tormenting flames**" (1.5.3) of hell to deliver its message. This is appropriate because it's the Ghost that inspires Hamlet's **madness**.

4) Alternatively, **metaphors** create a **stronger link** between **separate ideas** by saying something **is** something else:

- When Hamlet says that "**Denmark's a prison**" (2.2.243) he uses a **metaphor** to **emphasise** the sense of **claustrophobia** he feels in the court. The **image** of the **prison** works on several levels.
- Shakespeare **uses** layers of metaphors when he shows Hamlet in competition with Rosencrantz and Guildenstern. In a fast-paced exchange, the **world** becomes a **prison**, in which **Denmark** is one of the "**worst**" **cells** (2.2.246). Rosencrantz picks up the **metaphor** and says that the prison is in Hamlet's "**mind**" to which Hamlet replies that it's his "**bad dreams**" which **imprison** him (2.2.252-255).

When Images are Repeated they become a Motif

1) Shakespeare returns to the same **images** to **build up** a **theme** or a '**leitmotif**' that runs through the play.

2) A **recurring image** of **rot** and **disease** makes Denmark and its court seem **infected** with **sin**:

- Marcellus predicts that "**Something is rotten**" in Denmark (1.4.90).
- Claudius says that "**my offence is rank. It smells to heaven**" (3.3.36), which suggests that his sin is like a dead body.
- Hamlet uses a **simile** to **compare** Claudius to a "**mildewed ear**" (3.4.65), which **reminds** the **audience** of the **method** of **Claudius's crime**.

Look at the glossary on p.78-79 for definitions of more literary techniques.

Shakespeare uses Symbols to Emphasise the Themes

1) A symbol is an **object** that represents an **idea** or **theme**. It can either be **present** on the **stage**, or just mentioned by a **character**.

2) This technique helps the audience associate some of the **attributes** of the **object** with the **idea** it's trying to convey:

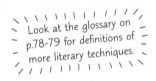

Flower symbolism is the idea that different flowers symbolise certain things e.g. rosemary stands for remembrance.

- When Ophelia gives out **flowers** in Act 4, Scene 5, she refers to **traditional** flower symbolism: "**There's rosemary, that's for remembrance**" (4.5.176). Kenneth Branagh's film of *Hamlet* shows Ophelia handing out **imaginary** flowers to **emphasise** their status as **symbols**, as well as **evidence** of her **madness**.
- **Yorick's skull** represents **three things** in one: it's literally part of the **remains** of Yorick, it's a **reminder** of what Yorick was like when he was **alive** and it's a **symbol** of **death** where the 'face' of **death** is **looking back**. The skull is a **symbol** for the **inevitability** of death (for more on *memento mori* see p. 48).

Imagery

Shakespeare *Personifies* some of his *Abstract Ideas*

1) Personification is used to **describe objects**, **ideas** or **animals** as if they have **human qualities**.
   It's a type of **metaphor** because the object is described as if it is human.

   - In his soliloquy in Act 2, Scene 2 Hamlet addresses '**O, vengeance!**' (2.2.579) as if it is a
     spiritual being. This is in the style of the **Ancient Roman** and **Medieval** plays in which **abstract
     ideas** such as **Time** or **Fortune** would be played by an actor. Hamlet plays on this **tradition** with
     Rosencrantz and Guildenstern when they discuss **parts** of **Fortune's body** — he uses **vulgar
     puns** to suggest they "**live about her waist, or in the middle of her favours**" (2.2.231-232).
   - Hamlet personifies a **recorder** in Act 3, Scene 2. He describes **playing** the recorder as giving
     it "**breath with your mouth**" (3.2.366) to suggest it can take part in "**discourse**" (conversation)
     (3.2.367). Hamlet then uses this personified recorder to **imagine** the **opposite** — himself as
     a **recorder**. He tells Rosencrantz and Guildenstern that they would "**play upon me... would
     seem to know my stops**" (3.2.372-373). Hamlet personifies the recorder and objectifies
     himself to show how he feels about Rosencrantz and Guildenstern **manipulating** him.

2) Shakespeare uses personification to give added **power** and **meaning** to
   the play's **dialogue** — it **increases** the **impact** of the language that he uses.

Imagery *Reveals More* than what the *Audience* can *See On Stage*

1) **Imagery**, **metaphor**, **simile** and **personification** are important and **functional**
   parts of **Shakespearean theatre**. With limited **props**, **scenery** and **lighting**,
   Elizabethan stages were **blank** and **open spaces** that actors had to **transform**
   into scenes using **descriptive language** and **convincing action**.

   - **Imagery enhances** the scene for the **audience**.
   - **Metaphor** and **simile** make use of **objects**
     and **experiences familiar** to the audience.
     This helps the audience to **connect** them
     to a **new** or **unfamiliar** scene on stage.
   - **Personification** and **symbolism** allow actors
     to introduce **abstract ideas** without losing the
     understanding or **attention** of the **audience**.

© Alastair Muir/Rex Features

2) Without these techniques, it could be **difficult** for the audience to **imagine**
   the **scene** in all its detail and to **identify** with the characters on the **stage**.

Practice Questions

Q1 Read Laertes's lament in Act 4, Scene 7, lines 185-191. Underline and identify
    all the examples of imagery, metaphor, simile and personification in this extract.

Q2 Rewrite Laertes's lament in plain prose without any imagery. E.g. "Too much of water hast thou, poor Ophelia" would
    become "You have drowned, poor Ophelia". How does the tone of Laertes's lines change when you do this?

Q3 Horatio warns Hamlet that "The very place puts toys of desperation, / Without more motive, into every brain /
    That looks so many fathoms to the sea / And hears it roar beneath." (1.4.75-78).
    What is the effect of his use of imagery here? Refer to specific literary techniques in your answer.

"Mad as the sea and wind when both contend / Which is the mightier"

Some of Shakespeare's metaphors and similes have been absorbed into the language, so you might not spot them at first.
The phrase "mind's eye" (1.1.112) is an example of personification that might need a second glance before you realise.

Cultural Context

Here's a bit of context for you before we get into the critical responses. If you have any critical responses, such as "my book is sticky", "I don't like the colours on page xx" or "your book came to life and bit me" please visit our website...

'Hamlet' was Written at a time when Theatre was Changing

1) **Before** the Renaissance, there were **no theatre companies**, plays were quite **short** and were usually **religious**.

2) The Renaissance **encouraged dramatists** to focus on the **Classical drama** of the Greeks and the Romans. They started to take **old texts** and **re-work** them — people who went to see plays **expected** to know the **plot** but hoped to see a **skilled playwright** introduce **new elements** to the story.

3) As a result, plays got **longer** and were **inspired** by **history** and **legend**. *Hamlet* took its **inspiration** from **two main sources** — *Ur-Hamlet* and *Amleth*. *Ur-Hamlet* was based on the older story of *Amleth*, a **popular folk story** in Scandinavia, that was written by Danish historian **Saxo Grammaticus** (see p.52).

Shakespeare was Writing in a Renaissance

> The Renaissance was a cultural movement inspired by the Classical arts that took place between the 14th and 17th century.

1) The Renaissance was 'a **rebirth**' of artistic and intellectual interests which **challenged old traditions**. The **rediscovery** of **Ancient Classical texts** made people **rethink** what **man** was **capable of achieving**.

2) **New** (and **original**) **ideas** were **encouraged** — **Copernicus** and **Galileo** proved that the **sun** was the **centre of the universe**. This challenged the idea that **humanity** (the Earth) was the most **important** part of **God's creation**.

3) **Shakespeare** also started to **challenge traditional values** — for example he made figures of **authority** (like Polonius) into **fools**, whilst **commoners** (such as the Gravedigger) frequently **outsmarted** their **social superiors**.

4) The **uncertainty** in *Hamlet* represents the **Renaissance belief** that everything should be **questioned** — Shakespeare was part of the developing **revenge tragedy genre** but he gave it a unique **twist**. He made his revenger more **philosophical** — Hamlet **delays** his revenge because of his **uncertainty**, rather than because of **physical restrictions**, which was the case in Kyd's *The Spanish Tragedy* (see p.42).

The Renaissance and Humanism came Hand in Hand

1) **Humanism** was a **school of thought** that embraced **Renaissance ideas**. Humanists **emphasised** the use of **reason** and focused on **improving mankind's abilities** as **far as possible**.

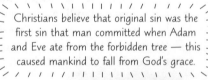

> Christians believe that original sin was the first sin that man committed when Adam and Eve ate from the forbidden tree — this caused mankind to fall from God's grace.

2) Some humanists believed that **original sin** was caused by the **failure of reason**. They argued that Adam's **love** for Eve made him **give in** to **sin** — this could explain why **Hamlet** values **reason over passion**.

3) The **writings** of **famous humanists** could have influenced the **ideas** in *Hamlet*.

- The play seems to reflect the ideas about **ambiguity** and **uncertainty** in **Michel de Montaigne's** essays. Montaigne's **motto** was "**What do I know?**", an idea which seems to **inspire** many of **Hamlet's soliloquies**.

- Montaigne also wrote a lot about the **unreliable human experience**. He thought that man can only **experience** an **appearance of reality**, rather than the **truth** behind it. Similarly, Hamlet wants **revenge** for his father when he can **never know** the **full truth** about his **murder**.

- Hamlet's **speech** in **Act 2, Scene 2** that begins, "**What a piece of work is a man**" (lines 303-310) is **based upon** *The Oration on the Dignity of Man*, a work by a **well-known Italian humanist**, **Pico della Mirandola**.

Michel de Montaigne (1533-1592)

4) The play also **reflects** the **general feelings of scepticism** encouraged by Elizabethan humanists. Hamlet **questions** Horatio's **beliefs** and **general philosophy** saying, "**There are more things in heaven and earth, Horatio, / Than are dreamt of in your philosophy**" (1.5.166-167). **Humanists** took **nothing for granted** and **questioned everything** in the same way that Hamlet does.

Cultural Context

'Hamlet' was *Influenced* by the *Protestant Reformation*

1) Shakespeare **addresses widespread concerns** about death in *Hamlet* — it's considered his **most Christian** play because **Hamlet** is so **preoccupied** with **death**, the **afterlife** and his **soul**. The new **Protestant beliefs** at the time were **confusing** for many and they also **removed** the idea of **purgatory**. This meant that a lot of people were **worried** about whether they'd be **forgotten** after death (see p.41).

> The Protestant Reformation was well established in England under Elizabeth I. It replaced the old Catholic beliefs.

2) The Protestant Reformation made other **religious changes**. Protestants made an **individual's conscience** the **centre** of **religious life**. Shakespeare's **heroes** are often **haunted** by their **consciences** like Hamlet.

3) Some Protestants believed in **predestination**. This is the idea that **God** has planned **everything** — whatever you do, you **can't change** your **fate**. This **confused** a lot of people because they were also said to have **free will** and that they were in **control** of their **own salvation**. In the play, Hamlet seems to **believe** in **predestination**, but refers to it as **"providence"** (5.2.214). Providence is basically a Christian word for **fate**.

> **Contemporary Commentary**
>
> The fact that Hamlet **studies** at the **University of Wittenberg** is **important** — Wittenberg was the **birthplace** of **Lutheranism** (a type of **Protestantism**) and a centre of **humanism**.

'Hamlet' Reflects the *Social Concerns* of the time

> Censoring means removing or changing anything that's thought to be dangerous or harmful.

SOCIAL UNREST

1) The **Renaissance** and **Reformation** made the English people **confused** and **restless**. The **monarchy** was **concerned** that **playwrights** like Shakespeare might spread **radical ideas** and they **censored** anything that was seen as **dangerous**. Plays were used to **provoke unrest** — Shakespeare's company performed *Richard II* (a play about **removing a monarch**) on the night before the **1601 rebellion** against Elizabeth I. Some **historicists** have suggested that *Hamlet* is also about **challenging** the **monarchy** (see p.69)

2) It's been argued that *Hamlet* was **censored** — the line **"There is special providence in the fall of a sparrow"** (5.2.213-214) was originally written as **"There's a predestinate providence"**. Even though this was a **Protestant** belief, Puritans were **worried** that **people** would use **predestination** to **justify immoral actions** by saying that **God** had **made them** do it.

GENDER ROLES

1) **Women** were **financially dependent** on first their **father** and then their **husband** when they **married**. They had very **few rights** of their own and were seen as **less intelligent** than men.

2) Women were expected to be **virgins** until **marriage** and **remarried less often** than men did. It was also **forbidden** to marry your **brother's wife** in the Book of Common Prayer.

3) **Doctors** in Shakespeare's time **genuinely believed** that **love** caused **insanity**. **Bernard of Gordon** wrote in his **medical encyclopedia** that **"melancholy anguish"** or madness is **"caused by love for a woman"**.

Practice Questions

Q1 Michel de Montaigne wrote "I put forward formless and unresolved notions... not to establish the truth but to seek it". Assess whether Hamlet seeks or establishes the truth in at least two of his soliloquies.

Q2 Niccolò Machiavelli wrote that "men are driven by two principal impulses, either by love or by fear". Explore this idea in an analysis of the major characters in *Hamlet*. Give examples to back up your answer.

"Sticking to one's own opinions is the surest proof of stupidity" — Montaigne

Michel de Montaigne also said "In true education, anything that comes to our hand is as good as a book: the prank of a pageboy, the blunder of a servant... they are all part of the curriculum." I tried telling that to the examiner but they weren't having any of it...

Early Critics

They say the early bird catches the worm, but the second mouse gets the cheese. Early critics are more like the early mouse than the bird. They thought they had Hamlet's worm, but the critics that came after them actually got the cheese...

Neoclassicism *looked again at* Ancient Plays

Neoclassical critics compared contemporary drama to the classical works the playwrights were trying to imitate.

Neoclassicists compared Shakespeare's tragedies with ancient classical drama as well as Aristotle's dramatic theory in his *Poetics*. Neoclassicists, like 17th century critics Thomas Rymer and Jeremy Collier, wanted tragedies to have tragic decorum — this meant that:

- Plot was key — there had to be a single plot line and events had to occur in a limited time and space.
- The characters (and women in particular) had to act politely and contribute to the plot's action.
- The language also had to be appropriate — crude words weren't acceptable.
- The play and its characters had to have a moral focus.

See p.54 for more on Aristotle's tragic theory.

Neoclassicists also emphasised the role of poetic justice — the characters had to get what they deserved. This was an idea that wasn't important in Aristotle's *Poetics*.

17th Century Criticism *looked at* Shakespeare's Language

Hamlet was popular with Shakespeare's contemporaries — it was one of his most performed plays. His contemporaries weren't concerned with the play's ambiguities like many modern critics are now.

1) The Puritans had shut the theatres from 1640-1660. When they reopened, productions of *Hamlet* exaggerated the violent aspects of the play which appealed to the masses, such as Hamlet's madness and the Ghost.

2) Criticism of the play was usually aimed at Shakespeare himself, who was seen as primitive. He wasn't as educated as many other playwrights, and many critics thought that the play was too lowbrow.

- John Evelyn wrote that "the old plays begin to disgust this refined age" — he criticised the violent scenes in the play. Evelyn also questioned whether *Hamlet* had a clear sense of justice.
- *Hamlet's* crude and bawdy language was also criticised, especially Polonius's use of puns and Hamlet's sexually charged expressions, such as "Do you think I meant country matters?" (3.2.125).
- Jeremy Collier was a respected critic at the time who challenged the play's immorality and foul language. He condemned Shakespeare for making Ophelia "immodest" when she goes insane.

3) *Hamlet* was defended by Thomas D'Urfey and George Drake:

- Drake argued that there was justice in the play because the murderers are "caught in their own toils" (their own traps) and that Ophelia's immodesty was reasonably explained by her desperate state.
- D'Urfey simply argued that critics had found immorality in places where there was none.

18th Century Critics *questioned the play's* Morality

1) Early 18th century critics continued to criticise the violence of the play and its sexual and religious immorality:

- Voltaire called *Hamlet* "the fruit of the imagination of a drunken savage".
- Dr Johnson criticised particularly violent bits of the play. He called Hamlet's soliloquy in Act 3, Scene 3 "too horrible to be read or to be uttered" as it was so merciless.
- Johnson also questioned whether Hamlet had to treat Ophelia so cruelly. He thought that the play's ending was unrealistic and unsatisfactory.

Dr Samuel Johnson (1709-1784)

2) Despite this, *Hamlet* was more popular with 18th century critics than 17th century critics. The parts of the play that broke tragic decorum were seen as a strength of Shakespeare's writing rather than a weakness.

3) Horace Walpole defended the mixture of comic and tragic elements in *Hamlet* as being more believable than a straight tragedy and Aaron Hill praised the contradictions in Hamlet's character, saying that it made him more lifelike. Critics began to see the play as less of a dramatic work and more of a psychological study.

Romanticism

'I love you book.' 'I love you too printer GB05.' 'It's nice when you call me pet names.' 'Feel like making out?' 'Er... not really. I always get paper cuts.' 'Pah! How romantic.' 'I'm sorry book. How about I tell you about Romanticism instead...'

Romanticism was a Reaction Against Scientific Reason

Romantic criticism analysed **characters' psychological states** and the **relationships** between them.

1) **Romanticism** was an **intellectual movement** in the late 18th century and early 19th century. Romantics focused on **beauty** and the **individual**, and encouraged people to value their **emotions**.

2) The critics in this period were **less concerned** by Shakespeare's **language** than previous critics and looked mainly at the **character** of **Hamlet** and his **psychological state**.

3) Romantic critics were usually **authors** who wrote about how the individual could be affected by things like **isolation**, **melancholy**, and **personal misery**. This meant that they could **relate** to Hamlet — **Coleridge** saw a **"smack of Hamlet"** in himself, whilst **Keats** is said to have read *Hamlet* **40 times**.

4) Romantic critics greatly **admired** Shakespeare — anyone who **questioned** his brilliance tended to be **alienated** by the **critical community**.

Romantic Critics Linked Hamlet's Delay to his Intellect

1) The Romantics preferred to study the play as a **text**, rather than a **dramatic production** like the **neoclassicists**. **William Hazlitt** said that **"There is no play that suffers so much in being transferred to the stage"**.

2) Romantic critics started considering the **issue** of Hamlet's **delay** for the **first time**. They believed that Hamlet's **impressive intellect** explained his delay and that his **hesitation** was **important** to his **character**.

3) **Goethe** suggested that Hamlet can't **balance** his **thoughts** and **actions** because he's so highly intelligent. In other words Hamlet can't **reconcile** his **morality** with the **horrible act** that he's been asked to commit.

4) Similarly, **Samuel Coleridge** argued that *Hamlet* was a **psychological study** of an **over-imaginative** person with an **unwillingness to act** — basically, Hamlet **thinks too much**, and can't **make up his mind**. Coleridge also argued that the play's **message** was that we should **act**, rather than **delay**. He praised *Hamlet* for raising serious **philosophical questions** which encouraged the **audience** to **grow intellectually**.

5) The Romantics' treatment of the **character** of Hamlet as **separate** from the **text** made them realise that his **complexities** made him **lifelike** — he couldn't be easily **summed up**, just like a **real person**.

Even though Hamlet's a **deep intellectual thinker**, Coleridge and Hazlitt also argued that Hamlet was an **'everyman'** character — the play has such a **wide popularity** because everyone can see **themselves** in Hamlet. Hazlitt famously said, **"It is *we* who are Hamlet"**.

Practice Questions

Q1 Aristotle argued that characters should act according to the "law of probability or necessity". In other words, characters' actions should be shaped by "probability" (what most of us would do), or "necessity" (what they're 'forced' to do). Write a critique of *Hamlet* analysing whether the characters in the play follow this rule.

Q2 Dr Johnson wrote that Hamlet "makes no attempt to punish him [Claudius], and his [Claudius's] death is at last effected by an incident which Hamlet has no part in producing". To what extent do you agree with this statement?

Q3 William Hazlitt wrote that "Hamlet is as little of the hero as a man can well be". To what extent do you agree with this statement? Refer to the text in your answer.

"He [Hamlet] is the most amiable of misanthropes*" — William Hazlitt

I know what you're thinking — these Romantics sound an awful lot like modern day emos. Well they are, sort of. They're like distant cousins, twice removed. The only difference is, instead of singing about how they weren't okay, they wrote about it.

*misanthrope = someone who generally dislikes humankind

20th Century Criticism

Yes, finally. What we've all been waiting for... a page on Sigmund Freud. I actually made a Freudian slip the other day — it was really embarrassing. It just goes to show that you shouldn't leave banana skins lying around willy-frilly.

Psychoanalytic Approaches look at the Characters' Minds

> **Psychoanalytic critics** examine the characters' **repressed desires** and search for **hidden messages** in the text's **imagery** and **symbolism**.

Psychoanalyst approaches inspired Laurence Olivier's 1947 film to internalise Hamlet's soliloquies as voice-overs.

1) **20th century criticism** of Hamlet was **mainly concerned** with **character analysis**. Critics attempted to **explain** Hamlet's **delay**, which was considered the play's **main weakness**.

2) **Sigmund Freud** produced **new psychoanalytic theories** to try to explain the **mysteries** of **human behaviour** by analysing the **unconscious mind**. These theories began to be **applied** to texts like *Hamlet*.

Freud's main evidence is Act 3, Scene 4 but critics have argued that Hamlet's language here isn't lustful but more similar to that of a preacher — it's full of religious references.

Freud's Oedipal Analysis

1) Freud believed that the **unconscious mind** was full of **thoughts, feelings** and **memories** that people were **unaware** of but that **influenced** their **behaviour**.

2) In his book *The Interpretation of Dreams*, Freud **rejected** Goethe's idea that Hamlet's **high intelligence** prevented him from acting. Freud argued that Hamlet **can take action** because he **murders** Polonius, Rosencrantz and Guildenstern.

3) Freud argued that Hamlet's **hesitation** comes from his **unconscious mind**, because Hamlet has a **repressed desire** for his **mother**. This idea has **influenced** many **modern performances** of the **closet scene** in **Act 3, Scene 4** (such as Zeffirelli's 1990 film).

4) Freud suggested that Claudius **achieves** what Hamlet **subconsciously wished** he had done (**killing** his **father** and **sleeping with** his **mother**). Hamlet sees himself **mirrored** in his uncle and **doesn't want** to kill a part of **himself**.

Sigmund Freud
1856-1939

© Mary Evans Picture Library/Imagno

Erlich's Father Figure Analysis

1) **Avi Erlich**, an English Literature professor and psychotherapist, **didn't agree** with Freud's approach. He **questioned** whether Freud was just **imposing** his own **beliefs** about the **Oedipus Complex** on the play.

2) Erlich argued that every boy needs a **strong father** who they can **imitate** and he believed that Hamlet's **psychological problems** are caused by the **lack** of this **strong father figure**. He argued that Hamlet **wants to believe** that his father was a **strong man** but **suspects** that he was **weak** — this could explain why Shakespeare **questions** the **reliability** of Hamlet's **memory** in the play.

3) Erlich explained that the **delay** occurs because Hamlet wants his **weak father** to be **strong** and take his **own revenge**, rather than getting his **son** to do it **for him**.

A.C. Bradley Focused on Character Criticism

A.C. Bradley's approach to *Hamlet* focused on the **character** of Hamlet and his **actions**.

1) Like the neoclassical critics, Bradley thought that the plot should be **unified**. However, he believed that tragedy comes mainly from **character** and the **character's actions**, rather than the **plot**.

2) Bradley argued that the **conflict** in *Hamlet* is a result of Hamlet's "**inward struggle**" — it comes from his **reluctance** to **fulfil** the **role** of the **traditional revenger** in a revenge tragedy.

3) Bradley saw this **reluctance** as Hamlet's reaction to his **circumstances**. Bradley didn't agree with the **Romantic idea** that Hamlet's **delay** is **explained** by his **over-developed intellect**. Instead, he argued that Hamlet is a "**man who at any *other* time and in any *other* circumstances... would have been perfectly equal to his task**". His **struggle** is partly caused by his inability to cope with the **position** he finds himself in.

4) **Bradley** argued that Hamlet's **lack** of action is caused by his **disgust** for his mother's **lustfulness**. Gertrude's actions and Hamlet's **sensitive nature** meant that he also became **disgusted** with the **world**, and this stopped him from acting.

20th Century Criticism

Some Critics Rejected the Psychoanalytic Approach

1) **Some critics** pointed out that **psychoanalytic approaches** were **problematic** because they treat the characters like **real people** and **ignore artistic concerns**.

2) **T.S. Eliot's** essay 'Hamlet and His Problems', **disagreed** with the **Romantic's idealisation** of Shakespeare, and instead suggested that it was the **play** that was the **problem** — Hamlet's delay was the result of "**an artistic failure**".

3) Eliot **questioned** Hamlet's **believability** as a character and argued that it was **difficult** to **understand** his **behaviour**. He also thought that the play did not **accurately** reflect **real life**.

4) Eliot also thought that Hamlet's **reaction** to Gertrude was **excessive** for her **crimes** — he thought that her character was too "**insignificant**" to have had a **substantial impact** on the play's **events**. Eliot **disagreed** with **Bradley's claim** that Gertrude was to **blame** for causing Hamlet's **disgust** with the world and ultimately his **delay**.

5) **C.S. Lewis** is another critic who **refused** to analyse Hamlet as an **individual**. He argued that, although Shakespeare doesn't make the **reasons** for Hamlet's delay **clear**, it **doesn't matter**. Lewis thought that **character analysis** missed the **point** of the play, which is to **examine** the **mystery of human existence**.

6) Lewis argued that, in the character of Hamlet, Shakespeare **successfully created** a realistic everyman character who is haunted by **original sin** and **fear of death** and denied that the play was a **failure**.

Performance Critics study the play as a Theatrical Production

Performance critics consider plays as they're **performed** rather than looking at them as **literary works**.

1) Because *Hamlet* is so **popular**, it's been **performed** and **interpreted** in many **different ways**. This led critics such as **Harley Granville-Barker** to focus on the more **dramatic elements** of the play.

2) Granville-Barker **focused** on how Shakespeare builds **dramatic tension** in the play — in one of his essays 'Place-structure and Time-structure' he looks at how **location** and **time** are used **effectively** for this **purpose**:

LOCATION
- Barker argues that Shakespeare **focuses** on **Elsinore** as the **centre** of the **play's action** and so the **scenes outside** of the castle (e.g. the pirate's rescue, Laertes in Paris) are **rarely performed** on **stage**. Barker argues that this is a **dramatic decision**, and that Shakespeare could have allowed these scenes to **play out** on stage, as **talking** about the events takes just as **long** as **showing them**.
- Shakespeare **concentrates** the **action** at Elsinore to **highlight** Hamlet's **tragic inability** to take **action**. Other people **come** and **go** but Hamlet isn't **involved** — he only **leaves** for England when he's **ordered** to.

TIME
- Barker points out that plays usually **ignore time** or use **act divisions** to **indicate** the **passing of time**. In *Hamlet,* Shakespeare uses time only when he thought it was **dramatically necessary**.
- By Act 3 Shakespeare **doesn't mention** the passing of time at all — this helps the **audience** to identify with **Hamlet**, as he **loses track** of time as well (see p.55). It also helps sustain the **play's illusion** that the events of the play are happening in **real time** so it seems more **realistic**.
- As the play's action reaches a **climax**, events seem to happen more **quickly** and the **time frame** becomes noticeably **smaller**, particularly in **Act 4**. This **builds tension** for the **audience**.

Practice Questions

Q1 Freud's argument that Hamlet has a repressed desire for his mother mostly takes its evidence from the 'closet scene' in Act 3, Scene 4. Analyse this scene in detail and decide whether or not it supports this argument.

Q2 C.S. Lewis argues that "the subject of *Hamlet* is death". Do you think that this is a fair assessment of the play? By referring to the text in your answer, explain what you think is the subject of the *Hamlet*.

"Hamlet the play is the primary problem" — T.S. Eliot

There's a reason T.S. Eliot didn't try his hand at writing musicals. 'How do you solve a problem like O-phee-liaa? Answer — You can't.' I wonder how he'd like it if we said that his work was basically rubbish like he did with Shakespeare... the big meanie-pants.

Feminism

I thought I was a feminist for many years... and then I realised it was Gemini, not Femini. Silly me. It's not as bad as my friend Dave, he thought he was an Aquarium. Sad story... but he's been taken somewhere safe now.

Feminism Focuses on the Female Characters

Feminist critics are concerned with the **presentation** of **women** in literature.

1) In the **Elizabethan era**, **women** were **classified** by their **sexuality** — they could be categorised as **virgins**, **wives**, **widows** or **whores**. Feminist critics tend to **defend** Gertrude and Ophelia, and try to **explain** why the **female characters** seem **less developed** than the **male characters**.

2) Feminists also **challenge** the **traditional view** that the female characters only have **value** because they aid the **development** of the **male characters**. Traditionally, **character analysis** of the men in *Hamlet* focuses on the **male characters themselves**, but analysis of Gertrude and Ophelia **focuses** largely on their **relationships** with men.

They Defend Ophelia's Character...

Some of the **areas** that **feminist critics** look at when **studying** Ophelia's character are:

DOUBLE STANDARD

1) Feminists argue that the **treatment** of Ophelia represents the Elizabethan **double standard**. They agree with her comments that the **men** who **control** her life are **hypocrites** and do what they **want** (1.3.44-49).

2) Ophelia's initial independence in **Act 1, Scene 3**, when it's revealed that she's seen Hamlet **alone**, is **repressed** by Polonius and Laertes. Laertes is told to be **true** to **himself** but Ophelia is warned not to **trust** her **own judgement**: "Think yourself a baby" (1.3.105). The **male world** denies her any **independence**.

MADNESS

1) **Elaine Showalter** argues that Ophelia's **madness** highlights the **sexism** in the **Elizabethan period**. **Madmen** were said to be 'melancholic', a symptom of an **intellectual** mind pushed **too far**, whilst **madwomen** were called 'hysteric', an **illness** associated with **disturbances** in the **womb**.

2) Showalter also **denies** that Ophelia's madness is caused by the **loss** of the **dominant men** who control her life. Psychoanalytic feminist critics have instead argued that Ophelia goes mad with **guilt** because she **secretly** wants Hamlet to **kill her father** so that they can have a **relationship**.

3) Although Ophelia's madness suggests that she's a **victim**, some critics argue that her madness is a **rejection** of the **traditional male hierarchy** that forces **chastity** onto her. Some critics argue that **playwrights** used **madness** to **give women** a voice that they wouldn't otherwise have.

DEVELOPMENT

1) **Linda Bamber** argues that Ophelia's character isn't **fully developed** because she's simply an **artistic device** used to **indicate** Hamlet's **psychological state**. His **behaviour** towards her **changes** as he begins to **accept** the **inevitability** of his **fate** and his **quest** for **vengeance**.

2) Hamlet's anger at **women** is redirected at his **uncle** when he **returns** from England — Hamlet **embraces** Ophelia at her **funeral** and declares that he "loved Ophelia" (5.1.265).

...and Give Gertrude a More Important Role

1) Feminist critics have tried to show that Gertrude has an **active role** in the play, rather than simply being an **unwitting victim**. Many feminist critics **accept** the fact that Gertrude is **naïve** and that she does have **ambiguous morality**. However, feminists such as **Carolyn Heilbrun** present Gertrude as a **peacemaker** who **remarries** to **create stability**, and argued for her **right** to have **sexual desires**:

   • In her **first appearance** Gertrude tries to **reconcile** her **new husband** with her **son** to create stability in the court.
   • When Hamlet asks her **not to sleep** with Claudius again in **Act 3, Scene 4**, she **avoids** giving a **direct answer**. This could suggest that Gertrude **doesn't want** to **agree** to something that she **has to do**.

2) Some feminists also **reject** the idea that Gertrude's **sexuality** is so **important**. Critics such as **Bamber** **blame** this reading on critics who **accept** Hamlet's **accusations**, when there's **limited textual evidence**. She argues that "**the relationship that we see between Gertrude and Claudius is... never sexual at all**".

Historicism and Marxism

Art imitates life. At least that's what the historicists believe in a nutshell. That explains why whenever I paint I just end up with a picture of a lonely person sitting at a computer tapping away at a keyboard hoping someone, somewhere cares...

Historicism Examines the Context of a Text

> **Historicist critics** look at the **text** in **relation** to its **social, cultural, political, economic** and **religious background**. They try to work out how the text's **message** relates to the **wider historical context**.

1) Historicists such as **Stephen Greenblatt disagreed** with claims by people like **Ben Jonson** who said Shakespeare "**was not of an age, but for all time**". Greenblatt argued that "**nothing comes from nothing, even in Shakespeare**" and said that **every text** and **author** was **embedded** in the **social** and **cultural context** they were **produced** in.

2) Historicists **rejected** the **Romantic critics** who **idealised** the play and instead showed how the play was **embedded** in **Elizabethan England**. Historicists tried to **uncover** the **motivations** behind *Hamlet*, and establish why it seems so **unique**.

- **Greenblatt** argues that *Hamlet* was **addressing** the **Elizabethan fear** of being **forgotten** after **death** (see p.41).
- **Alan Sinfield** argues that the play was **shaped** by the **confusion** at the time of **conflicting Catholic** and **Protestant beliefs**. He said that the **early part** of the play is more **Catholic** (with the Ghost in **Purgatory**) but when Hamlet gives in to **fate** in **Act 5**, this is more **Protestant**, because it refers to **predestination**.
- **Catherine Belsey** argues that Shakespeare was trying to **break away** from the Classical tradition — in **Classical plays**, characters were **driven** by the **plot**, but Hamlet **resists** the **narrative** as he **delays** his **revenge**.
- Other critics argue that Hamlet's **introverted personality** was **shaped** by the **new self-awareness** introduced by the **Renaissance**. There was a **new focus** on the importance of the **individual**, an idea which is present in *Hamlet*.

Marxist Criticism looks at Social and Economic Influences

> **Marxist critics** look at the **politics** of a **text** to see how it's been **shaped** by **society** and **economics**.

1) Marxist critics **believe** that there is a **constant class struggle** between the **upper** and **lower classes** which can be **explored** through **texts** like *Hamlet*. They believe that all literature is a **product** of its **culture** and reveals **important social values**.

2) **Catherine Belsey** argues that *Hamlet's* **dramatic interest** lies in the **conflict of authority** and **power** in the play — Hamlet is a **prince** and **heir** to the throne yet he opposes those in **power**. She tries to work out how it **fits in** within the **wider class struggle**.

3) Belsey argues that the play was **written** at a **time** when the **absolute power** of the **monarchy** was being **tested** by the **rise of capitalism** and there was an **unspoken debate** about the **possibilities** of resisting a **monarch**.

4) Some Marxist critics believe that **Shakespeare** wasn't very **revolutionary**, and that *Hamlet's* focus on the Danish **royal family** rather than on a **topic** more **relevant** to the **lower classes**, just **re-establishes** the **traditional class hierarchy**.

Karl Marx
(1818-1883)

Practice Questions

Q1 Linda Bamber states that Hamlet is incapable of love. She argues that Hamlet threw himself into Ophelia's grave more as "an act of aggression against Laertes than of reconciliation with the dead Ophelia." To what extent do you agree with her assessment of Hamlet's relationship with Ophelia? Refer to the text in your answer.

Q2 By referring to the text in your answer, argue both for and against the idea that *Hamlet* was shaped by the context in which it was written. Write a conclusion explaining which argument you found more convincing and why.

"The madwoman is a heroine, a powerful figure" — Elaine Showalter

Regardless of the critical approach, critics tend to be very selective, ignoring passages which disprove their theories and heightening the importance of some scenes over others to make their point. Make sure you take their views with a pinch of salt, like my tears...

Writing About 'Hamlet'

Even though 'Hamlet' is a complicated play, there's no need for your essays to be incredibly complicated too. In fact, as with all essays, there's a simple but effective structure that you can follow in order to do well...

Use a *Plan* to *Structure* your *Argument*

1) **Before** you **start planning**, pick out the **key words** in the **question** so that you can **focus** on the most **important points**.

2) Once you've **worked out** exactly what the question's **asking**, you can start to **plan your argument**.

3) The **best essays** follow a **clear structure**:

- Your **introduction** should set out your **argument clearly** and **effectively** — it's the reader's **first impression** of your essay, so make sure it's a **good one**.

- Each **paragraph** should consider **one key point** of your **argument**. Don't try to cram everything into a couple of long paragraphs — you should consider **each point properly**.

- Every **paragraph** needs to **develop your answer** and each one should **follow on clearly** from the one before — this way your argument will be more **persuasive**.

- Your **conclusion** should **summarise** your **argument clearly** and **concisely**. Give a **final answer** to the **question** and **your personal response** to the text.

4) Plan your **argument** by making a **list** of **all** your **points** and the **evidence** that you're going to use to **back up** each one — this means that your argument will be **supported** all the way through.

5) Work out the **best order** to **tackle** your points so that the essay **flows naturally**. Try **linking** your **paragraphs** by placing **similar topics** next to each other — you could use **bullet points**, **tables** or **spider diagrams** to organise your ideas.

Use *Quotes* to *Back Up* your *Points*

Quoting from both the **play** and **critics** are good ways of **backing up** your **argument**:

If you're quoting from the **play**, **analyse** the quotes, rather than simply **listing** them. Tell the reader what it **shows** and how it **supports your argument**. Avoid using **long quotes** with lots of **ellipses**.

Some critics claim that Hamlet is misogynistic, but actually he's just disgusted by his mother's sexuality: "Why, she would hang on him / As if increase of appetite had grown / ... Frailty, thy name is woman".

Some critics argue that Hamlet is misogynistic as he says, "Frailty, thy name is woman". However, Hamlet does not hate all women. He's just disgusted by his mother's behaviour as it "blurs the grace and blush of modesty".

Be **selective** if you're quoting a **critic** — it shows your reader that you're using a critic's argument to make a **valid point**. It also shows that you **understand** that it's the **argument** that's **important**, and not the fact that you can **remember** lots of **quotes**.

Elaine Showalter says that "For most critics of Shakespeare, Ophelia has been an insignificant minor character in the play... chiefly interesting, of course, in what she tells us about Hamlet".

Elaine Showalter argues that Ophelia has not been properly studied as a character in her own right, and that she has only been considered in terms of "what she tells us about Hamlet".

You need to make **critical quotes part** of your argument rather than simply using them **as your argument**. Don't be afraid to **challenge** critical views with your **own opinions**. You can **evaluate** the **strengths** and **weaknesses** of **critical approaches** as you **develop** your **answer**. Remember that if you're writing an **undergraduate essay** you'll need to **reference** your critics **properly**.

Writing About 'Hamlet'

CULTURAL AND HISTORICAL CONTEXT	Look at the **influences** that **shaped** the **text** and the **author's opinions** and **writing style**. Consider how the context would have **affected** the **audience** it was written for. Read some **historicist critics** to **understand** the **importance of context** (see p.69).
ANALYSING FORM AND STRUCTURE	Look at the **genre** (e.g. whether it's a **tragedy** or a **comedy**) and its **form** (e.g. a **play** instead of a **poem** or **novel**) and look at how they've **affected** the way the text is **written**. When looking at the **structure**, you should **consider** how the **plot unfolds**, how the text is **shaped** by **stanzas**, **scenes** and **act divisions** as well as the **setting** and **passing of time** (see p.55).
CLOSE ANALYSIS OF LANGUAGE	Look at **short extracts** or **scenes** to **analyse** the **language** that the author uses to **create** a **certain effect**. This could involve looking at things like **wordplay**, **rhythm** and **alliteration**.
A RANGE OF CRITICAL OPINIONS	Consider **different critical approaches** to the text, **analyse** their **arguments** and decide if you **agree** or **disagree** with them. **Critical opinion** is a useful way to **support** your arguments.
THE RELATIONSHIP BETWEEN DIFFERENT TEXTS	Look at **other works** that share the **same form** or **themes** and see how **other authors** approach them. It's also **helpful** to look at **other works** by the **same author**.

A-Level Examiners Look at Four Main Skills...

These Assessment Objectives are for A-Level English Literature only.

To get **top marks** at **A-level** you need to make sure that you **understand** and **meet** the **assessment objectives**. Assessment objectives are **helpful little clues** that tell you what the **examiners** want to see in **your work**:

(1) Assessment Objective 1 — AO1

You need to write **clearly**, **accurately** and with **good spelling**. Your work must show **creative thought**, **answer the question**, and be **backed up** with a good **knowledge** of the **text**. You should use **technical terms** where it's **appropriate** (e.g. iambic pentameter, blank verse, soliloquy).

(2) Assessment Objective 2 — AO2

You need to **analyse** in **detail** how **structure**, **form** and **language** create **meanings** in the text.

(3) Assessment Objective 3 — AO3

You need to **compare** and **contrast different texts** with one another. You should give a **reasonable personal response** to the different texts as well as taking into account **other interpretations**.

(4) Assessment Objective 4 — AO4

You need to **understand** how **context** might have **influenced** the text. **Explain** the **impact** of the **historical**, **cultural** and **literary** context on the **author** and the **audience**.

Important info: If you're doing your exams from 2017 onwards, the Assessment Objectives will be slightly different. Please check with your teacher.

> English Language and Literature
>
> If you're studying *Hamlet* for **English Language and Literature**, you'll need to **focus** on how **different language** is used for different **purposes** and **audiences**. **Analyse** the text using the **ideas** that you've looked at in **integrated linguistic** and **literary studies**.

"The roots of education are bitter, but the fruit is sweet" — Aristotle...

My teacher told me this at school and cleverly I replied, 'But what if the fruit is a lemon?' The teacher wasn't too happy. The saying might work if you made the lemons into lemonade — 'The roots of education are bitter, but the fruity, carbonated sugary drink is sweet...'

Writing About 'Hamlet'

You might be doing an essay question on 'Hamlet' as a piece of coursework or in an exam.
This page deals mostly with an exam-type essay question, but it'll also be useful if you're doing coursework.

Pick out the Key Words in the Question

You could analyse how Shakespeare ties the ruler's morality to the corruption of his court and country (AO2).

Explore Shakespeare's presentation of the themes of corruption and morality.

Think about the dramatic techniques that Shakespeare has used to present morality and corruption (AO1/AO2).

These themes could be examined through comparisons with 'Macbeth' (AO3).

You could talk about the Christian morality in Elizabethan England (AO4).

You could talk about neoclassicists who argued that the play was immoral (AO3).

Introduce your Argument in the Introduction

Referring to the terms used in the question shows your answer is focused.

You might **start** like this:

> Shakespeare presents the themes of morality and corruption in 'Hamlet' by personifying them in the characters of Hamlet and Claudius. Hamlet's constant concern about the morality of murder is one of the main reasons he delays killing his uncle. In contrast, Claudius is completely corrupt and seems to feel little guilt for murdering his brother.

This introduces a new idea right at the beginning of the essay. The use of technical terms will also impress the assessor (AO1).

This introduction is **good** because it **sets the scene** for the rest of the essay — the **reader** knows that the essay will discuss the **characters** of **Hamlet** and **Claudius** and how they **represent** the themes of **morality** and **corruption**.

Make your First Paragraph about the most Important Point

The **first paragraph** should **expand** on the **points** made in the **introduction** more **fully**:

These short quotes show good textual knowledge and help support the argument (AO1).

> Even before Hamlet learns about his father's murder, he is aware of the corrupt nature of the court, comparing the world that he finds himself in to "an unweeded garden". In Hamlet's first soliloquy, Shakespeare establishes that Hamlet is separate from the corruption of the court, because he has a very strong morality. Though he wishes that "this too too sullied flesh would melt" he can't commit suicide because it goes against his Christian morals, as God fixed his "canon 'gainst self-slaughter".

This paragraph starts to provide **textual evidence** for **morality** in the play and so it **makes sense** to go on to provide **similar evidence** for **corruption** in the play and how Shakespeare uses Claudius to **represent** it:

This is good because it shows knowledge of the play's Christian context (AO4).

> Whereas Hamlet represents morality, Claudius represents corruption. Claudius is obsessed with gaining power and is willing to deceive others to preserve his position and manipulate people for his own gain. Hamlet describes Claudius's techniques as the "witchcraft of his wit" and as "traitorous gifts" to highlight his corruption. Shakespeare also links Claudius to corrupt Biblical characters to show his sinfulness. Claudius calls the murder of his brother the "primal eldest curse", which connects him with Cain (from the book of 'Genesis' in the Bible) who also killed his brother.

This paragraph provides a good case for Claudius **representing corruption** with plenty of **textual** evidence and **context**.

Writing About 'Hamlet'

Consider other Relevant Works

It's useful to think about **recurring themes** in other **Shakespeare plays** that can **back up** your **argument**.

> In many of Shakespeare's plays, such as 'Macbeth', characters are corrupted by their desire for power. Like Claudius, Macbeth kills the king so that he can take power. Both are selfish, but not necessarily evil. Both characters refuse to give up what they've gained from their crime, as shown when Claudius asks "May one be pardoned and retain th'offence?" Shakespeare makes it clear to the audience at the beginning of the play that Hamlet is separate from the corruption both visually with his mourning clothes of "nighted colour", and by presenting Hamlet as being opposed to the court's celebration.

This shows a good knowledge of other relevant works (AO3).

Consider the text as a play and analyse it from the perspective of the audience (AO4).

It's **important** that any **references** to other plays **add** to your **answer**. Some questions will ask you to **compare** Hamlet to **other works** (see p.74), so you'd need to **refer** to your comparison text **throughout** your essay.

Back Up your Points with Critical and Textual Knowledge

Use **critics** to **support** your argument, but don't be afraid to **challenge** their opinions if you **disagree**:

> Some neoclassicist critics argued that 'Hamlet' was an immoral play and that Shakespeare presented its protagonist, Hamlet, as having ambiguous morality. Dr Johnson thought that Hamlet's reasons for refusing to kill Claudius in prayer were "horrible" and that his treatment of Ophelia was unnecessarily cruel. However, this neoclassicist argument has been undermined by later critics who disagree that the play is immoral. They believed that the characters receive poetic justice because all of their crimes are paid for.

Using individual critics is good — you don't have to quote them directly but make sure you get their arguments right (AO3).

It would have been better to use a specific critic and go into more detail (AO3).

This is **good**, but rather than just **stating** a critic's opinion, you need to **develop** it and **analyse** it **yourself**:

> Critics such as George Drake criticised Dr Johnson's reading of 'Hamlet' and argued that there is a sense of morality in the play because all of the murderers are "caught in their own toils". All of the corrupt characters in the court die, such as Claudius and Polonius, as well as those characters who have ambiguous morality, like Hamlet and Gertrude. This suggests that Shakespeare was warning against the dangers of immorality and corruption.

This is much better because it **engages** with the critic and **applies** his view to the **text**.

Your Conclusion should Concisely Summarise your Argument

The conclusion doesn't need to introduce any **new ideas** but should put forward a **balanced answer** to the question:

This is good because it directly answers the question.

> Morality and corruption is a central theme in 'Hamlet' best symbolised by Shakespeare's presentation of the conflict between the moral Hamlet and the corrupt Claudius.
> A lot of Shakespeare's plays were concerned with the fact that power can corrupt. In 'Hamlet', Claudius is corrupted by his quest for power, and his corruption infects the court and makes Denmark "rotten". Whilst Hamlet does have ambiguous morality, his revenge ultimately removes the corruption, as it eventually results in Claudius's death. In this way, Shakespeare presents Hamlet's strong sense of morality, despite his internal struggle with what is right, as the antithesis of Claudius's absolute corruption.

This conclusion is **concise** and provides a **reasonable argument** that **answers** the **question**.

Comparing 'Hamlet'

'Hamlet' addresses so many of the major themes in literature that it can easily be compared to different texts. You'll need to consider things like genre, theme and language. If you're stuck for ideas, then this is the page for you...

How to **Compare Different** 'Hamlet' **Productions**

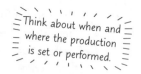
Think about when and where the production is set or performed.

1) If you're comparing **different productions** of *Hamlet*, it's a good idea to study some **performance criticism** to get an **idea** of the types of thing you can look at.

2) Every director of *Hamlet* has a **different interpretation** of the play, so there'll always be something to **compare** and **contrast**. You might consider:

- **What the production has cut out** — *Hamlet* is a **long play** and is **rarely performed** in its entirety. Looking at what a director cuts out **reveals** which **parts** they think are **more important**.
- **What the production has added in** — some productions **add scenes** or **dialogue** to make **more sense** of the **ambiguous elements** in the play. This shows what the **director** wants to **emphasise**.
- **How it presents the ambiguous issues** — some directors try to answer the **unanswered questions** by presenting scenes in a **certain way** e.g. **Zeffirelli's** film makes the scenes between Hamlet and Gertrude quite **sexual** to suggest that an **Oedipus complex** is a reason for Hamlet's **delay**.

3) It's useful to compare and contrast **different types** of production:

- **STAGE PRODUCTIONS** — look at how **scenery** and **props** are used to **change** the play's **focus** e.g. some productions use **modern settings** with things like **CCTV cameras** to **emphasise** the idea of **being watched**.
- **FILM PRODUCTIONS** — look at how films make the most of the fact that they aren't **limited** by the **stage**, e.g. **Olivier's** film turns Hamlet's **soliloquies** into **voice-overs** and **Branagh's** film uses **flashbacks**.
- **ADAPTATIONS** — *Hamlet* has been **remade** in **different ways**, e.g. Disney's *The Lion King*. Looking at how the play is **re-imagined** and placed in a **different context** is **interesting** and **raises new issues**.

How to **Compare** 'Hamlet' to other **Shakespearean Plays**

1) The easiest way to compare *Hamlet* with other **Shakespearean plays** is by looking at how Shakespeare **addresses** different **themes**. This shows how his **opinions** have **changed** over **time**.

2) Here are some **possible comparisons** you could make based on **themes** in *Hamlet*:

- **Revenge** (e.g. *The Merchant of Venice*, *The Tempest*) — Look at the **revenger's morality** and the issue of **delay**.
- **Madness** (e.g. *King Lear*, *Macbeth*) — Contrast Shakespeare's **presentation** of feigned and **real madness**.
- **Political Instability** (e.g. *Henry IV*, *Richard II*) — Analyse the **relationship** between the **ruler** and his **country**.
- **Suicide** (e.g. *Romeo and Juliet*, *Antony and Cleopatra*) — Consider the **different views** on the **morality** of **suicide**.
- **Murder** (e.g. *Titus Andronicus*, *Julius Caesar*) — Consider the **morality** and **consequences** of **murder**.
- **Dangers of Language** (e.g. *Othello*, *Richard III*) — Analyse how **language** is used to **manipulate** people.
- **Gender roles** (e.g. *Twelfth Night*, *The Taming of the Shrew*) — Look at how **gender stereotypes** are **addressed**.

3) Many **themes overlap** in Shakespeare's works, but this should give you an **idea** of the **links** you could make — there are plenty more **comparisons** and **plays** you could look at.

How to **Compare** 'Hamlet' to other **Tragedies**

1) *Hamlet* is **commonly compared** to Thomas Kyd's *The Spanish Tragedy* (see p.42), *Oedipus Rex* by **Sophocles** and *The Revenger's Tragedy* by Cyril Tourneur. Some of the **things** you could look at are:

- Tragic Flaws
- Fate versus Free Will
- Uncertainty and Doubt
- The Protagonist
- Delays
- Family Love
- Catharsis
- Reversals and Realisations.

2) **Aristotle's** *Poetics* is a **useful guide** for **comparing tragedies**. Aristotle **outlines** the **structure** and **qualities** of tragic drama — it was the **criteria** that **neoclassicists** used to **analyse** *Hamlet* originally (see p.64).

Comparing 'Hamlet'

Comparing 'Hamlet' to **Plays** of **Other Genres**

Think about comparing Shakespeare to other playwrights from the same era such as Christopher Marlowe.

TRAGICOMEDIES

- **Tragicomedies** have **elements** of **comedy** and **tragedy** in them.
- **Tom Stoppard's** *Rosencrantz and Guildenstern Are Dead* (see picture) is a tragicomedy. It's **based** on the **events** in *Hamlet* and **borrows** its **main characters** from **Shakespeare**.
- Stoppard's play **develops** *Hamlet's* **themes** of **fate** versus **free will**, the **inevitability** of **death** and **uncertainty** about truth.
- Stoppard's play was also **influenced** by the 'Theatre of the Absurd' — a **movement** in the 1950s when playwrights wrote about **Godless worlds**. Plays like *Waiting for Godot* and *Endgame* would provide a useful **third comparison** to Stoppard's play as well as *Hamlet,* and considering the **role of God** in the plays could be a good **starting point**.

© ODYSSEY / THE KOBAL COLLECTION

HISTORIES

- **History plays** draw their **inspiration** from **historical events**, especially times of **historical change.**
- Although they are **rooted** in **factual history**, history plays are **primarily designed** to **entertain** — they share a lot of the same **stylistic** and **artistic devices** as other plays. You could **consider** whether the **playwright** has tried to make their history play **fit** into the more **established tragic** and **comedic genres**.

There are many other **dramatic genres** — **approach comparisons** by looking at how the **writing style** is **different** from *Hamlet*.

How to **Compare** 'Hamlet' to **Other Forms** of **Literature**

Poetry

1) If you're comparing *Hamlet* to a **poem**, you could focus on the **different requirements** of the two **forms** (**play** and **poem**). So much of *Hamlet* is written in verse so you can make **form**, **style** and **language comparisons**.

2) Because poems are generally a lot **shorter** than *Hamlet,* you could **pick short extracts** from the play that share **similar themes** to the poem, but which provide a **good contrast** in terms of **language** and **style**.

3) Some of **Shakespeare's poems** such as his *Sonnets*, could provide an interesting **comparison**. Consider how **Shakespeare's writing** varies when he writes in a **different form**. You could explore Shakespeare's **attitude to women** in his **poetry** and **compare** it to his presentation of Ophelia and Gertrude.

Prose

CONTEMPORARY WORKS

- Comparing *Hamlet* with **works** from the **same era**, such as those written by **humanists**, puts the play in its **wider context**.
- A good way to approach comparisons with **humanist works** is to see how *Hamlet* **reflects** the **general mood** of the time and to **draw connections** between how the two texts **address similar issues**.
- You could consider how **'humanist'** *Hamlet* is and to **what extent** Shakespeare was **inspired** by **humanist texts** like **Thomas More's** *Utopia*, **Niccolò Machiavelli's** *The Prince* and **Montaigne's** *Essays*. Think about the effect of differences in **form** and **style**.

MODERN LITERATURE

- Some **themes** in *Hamlet*, such as **madness**, **love** and **revenge** are still **relevant** in modern literature. Other **issues** like **regicide** and **kingship** are **less common**.
- You could look at how **universal themes** like **love** and **death** relate to the **individual** in modern novels. For example, you could study **conflicts** between **parents** and **children**, feelings of **isolation** and **attitudes** towards **death**.
- You might also want to consider how the **ideas**, **attitudes** and **opinions** in *Hamlet* have **changed over time** e.g. you could look at how **women** are presented in modern literature.

Key Quotes

This page is a gift from me to you... if you've come this far then you deserve it. Use this page for inspiration when you can't quite remember that all-important quote or you need some ideas for a theme-based 'Hamlet' essay. Enjoy...

Important Quotes

HAMLET   My father's spirit! In arms! All is not well. / I doubt some foul play (1.2.255-256)

MARCELLUS   Something is rotten in the state of Denmark (1.4.90)

HAMLET   O my prophetic soul! / My uncle?
GHOST   Ay, that incestuous, that adulterate beast, / With witchcraft of his wit (1.5.40-43)

HAMLET   Denmark's a prison (2.2.243)   HAMLET   There's a divinity that shapes our ends (5.2.10)

HAMLET   Give me that man / That is not passion's slave, and I will wear him / In my heart's core (3.2.81-83)

CLAUDIUS O, my offence is rank. It smells to heaven. / It hath the primal eldest curse upon't (3.3.36-37)

Theme: Revenge

GHOST   Revenge his foul and most unnatural murder (1.5.25)

HAMLET   O, from this time forth, / My thoughts be bloody, or be nothing worth! (4.4.65)

CLAUDIUS What would you undertake / To show yourself in deed your father's son / More than in words?
LAERTES   To cut his throat i'th'church!
CLAUDIUS No place, indeed, should murder sanctuarize. / Revenge should have no bounds (4.7.123-127)

HAMLET   They are not near my conscience (5.2.58)

LAERTES   I am justly killed with mine own treachery (5.2.301)

Theme: Madness

HAMLET   To put an antic disposition on (1.5.172)

POLONIUS Though this be madness, yet there is method in't (2.2.205-6)

HAMLET   I am but mad north-north-west. When the wind is southerly, I know a hawk from a handsaw (2.2.377-378)

CLAUDIUS ...poor Ophelia / Divided from herself and her fair judgement (3.1.85-86)

CLAUDIUS Madness in great ones must not unwatched go (3.1.189)

HAMLET   Yet have I in me something dangerous, / Which let thy wisdom fear (5.1.258-259)

There are loads of other important quotes — have a look at Section 3 for more quotes relating to themes.

Key Quotes

Theme: Gender and Sexuality

HAMLET — Frailty, thy name is woman (1.2.146)

OPHELIA — 'Tis brief, my lord.
HAMLET — As woman's love. (3.2.162-163)

HAMLET — Get thee to a nunnery. Why wouldst thou be a breeder of sinners? (3.1.121-122)

HAMLET — God hath given you one face, and you make yourselves another (3.1.144-145)

Theme: Death

GERTRUDE — Thou knowest 'tis common. All that lives must die (1.2.72)

HAMLET — O that this too too sullied flesh would melt, / Thaw, and resolve itself into a dew (1.2.129-130)

HAMLET — I do not set my life at a pin's fee (1.4.65)

HAMLET — To be, or not to be — that is the question; / Whether 'tis nobler in the mind to suffer / The slings and arrows of outrageous fortune / Or to take arms against a sea of troubles (3.1.56-59)

HAMLET — For in that sleep of death what dreams may come (3.1.66)

HAMLET — Dost thou think Alexander looked o'this fashion i'th'earth?
HORATIO — E'en so (5.1.194-196)

Theme: Appearance and Reality

HAMLET — 'Seems', madam? Nay, it is. I know not 'seems' (1.2.76)

HAMLET — How weary, stale, flat, and unprofitable / Seem to me all the uses of this world! / Fie on't, ah, fie, 'tis an unweeded garden / That grows to seed (1.2.133-136)

HAMLET — ...methinks I see my father... / In my mind's eye, Horatio (1.2.184-185)

HAMLET — Be thou a spirit of health or goblin damned (1.4.40)

HAMLET — ...there is nothing either good or bad but thinking makes it so (2.2.248-249)

Critic Quotes

The poet is accused of having shown little regard to poetical justice, and... neglect of poetical probability. **Dr Johnson**

...the distresses of Hamlet are transferred... to the general account of humanity. **William Hazlitt**

Hamlet the play is the primary problem, and Hamlet the character only secondary. **T.S. Eliot**

Glossary

alliteration	When a **series** of words all start with the **same letter** or **sound**.
ambiguity	When a **word** or **idea** can be **interpreted** in **different** ways.
anaphora	The **repetition** of a **word** or **sequence of words** at the **beginning** of **nearby clauses** or **lines**.
antagonist	A **character** who provides the main **opposition** to the **protagonist**, e.g. Claudius.
antithesis	The **direct opposite** of something else, e.g. Gertrude is the antithesis of Hamlet.
apostrophe	A **rhetorical device** where the speaker addresses an **absent person** or **inanimate object**.
aside	When a **character** in a play **speaks** directly to the **audience**.
blank verse	**Unrhymed** verse in **iambic pentameter**.
caesura	A **pause** in a **line**, e.g. "To be, or not to be — that is the question."
catharsis	According to Aristotle, the **purging** of pity and fear that the **audience** feels at the end of a **tragedy**.
chorus	A **dramatic convention** used in **plays** to **narrate** the **plot** and comment on its **action**.
consonance	When words have the **same consonant sounds** but **different vowel sounds**, e.g. "tall / toil".
couplet	A **pair of lines** in **verse** that **rhyme** and have the **same rhythm**.
deus ex machina	An **unrealistic plot device** used to **solve problems** in a play.
everyman	A **character** that **represents** ordinary people.
feminism	In **literature**, a movement concerned with how **women** are **presented** by **writers**.
foils	A **character** who **contrasts** with the **protagonist**, a foil is used to emphasise some of the **main character's qualities** e.g. Laertes is a **foil** to Hamlet — Laertes's action highlights Hamlet's delay.
form	The **features** of a type of literature, such as its rhyme, rhythm or metre.
free will	The **power** to **act freely** without being **controlled** by **fate** or **God**.
genre	The **type** of literature, e.g. **drama**, **tragedy**. Hamlet is a **revenge tragedy**.
historicism	A **movement** that believes **historical context** is **vital** in order to **understand** a text.
homograph	Words that have the **same spelling** but a **different meaning**, e.g. bat (animal / sporting equipment).
homophone	Words that **sound the same** but have a **different meaning**, e.g. canon / cannon.
humanism	A **movement** that emphasised the use of **reason** and focused on **improving mankind's abilities**.
hyperbole	Deliberate **exaggeration** that's used to create a **dramatic effect**.
iambic pentameter	**Ten syllable lines** in which each **unstressed syllable** is followed by a **stressed syllable**.
imagery	**Figurative language** that creates a **picture** in your mind. It includes **metaphors** and **similes**.
introspective	The tendency to **inwardly examine** your own **mental** and **emotional state**.
irony	When words are used in a **sarcastic** or **comic way** to imply the **opposite** of what they normally **mean** or when there's a **big difference** between what people **expect** and what **actually happens**.
juxtaposition	Placing two things **next to each other** to create a **contrast**.

Glossary

Machiavellian	Being prepared to use **immoral behaviour** to gain or keep **power** — as based on the reputation of Niccolò Machiavelli.
memento mori	An **object** or symbol used to **remind** people that they will **die**.
metaphor	A way of **describing something** by saying that **it is** something else.
metatheatre	When a play **comments on itself**, drawing attention to the fact that it's a **play**.
metre	The arrangement of **stressed** and **unstressed syllables** to **create rhythm** in a **line of poetry**.
misogyny	A **general hatred** of **women**.
motif	A **repeated image** or **symbol**.
Neoclassicism	A **movement** that compared contemporary drama to **classical works**.
parody	A **speech** or **work** that **mocks** or **exaggerates** the features of another **speaker** or **literary style**.
pathos	A quality in a text which arouses **feelings** of **pity** or **sorrow** in the **reader** or **audience**.
personification	A kind of **metaphor** in which an **object** is described as if it's a **person** with **thoughts** and **feelings**.
predestination	A belief among some **Protestants** that God has **planned everything**.
protagonist	The **main character** of the work, e.g. Hamlet.
Protestant Reformation	The **Protestant movement** that took place in some countries which **replaced Catholic beliefs**.
providence	The idea that **God** looks after his **creation** and makes sure that things happen for the **best**.
Psychoanalytical	**Theories** which try to **explain human behaviour** by **analysing** the **unconscious mind**.
psychological	Relating to the **mental** and **emotional state** of a **person**.
pun	A **play on words** that uses **ambiguity** between words to create **humour**.
Renaissance	A **cultural movement** that took place between the 14th and 17th century.
rhetoric	The use of **language techniques** to make **speeches** or **writing** more powerful.
rhetorical question	Where a **question** is asked when the speaker doesn't **need** or **expect** a **reply**.
rhythm	A **pattern** of **sounds** created by the **arrangement** of **stressed** and **unstressed syllables**.
Romanticism	Beginning in the 18th century, a **movement** which valued **beauty**, **nature** and the **individual**.
sibilance	The **repetition** of the 'hissing' sounds in words, e.g. 'hush', 'serpent', 'gloss'.
simile	A way of **describing** something by saying that it's **like** something else.
soliloquy	A **character reveals** their **thoughts** and **feelings** when they're **alone** (or **think** they're alone) on stage.
Stoicism	An **emphasis** on **reason** over **emotion**, and the **enduring** of **hardships** without **complaint**.
superlative	Saying that something is the **most**, **least**, **best** or **worst** form of something.
symbol	When an **object stands for** something else, e.g. Yorick's skull is a symbol of death.
tone	The **mood** or **feelings** suggested by the **words** the writer uses.
tragic flaw	The **character flaw** of a **tragic hero** which leads to his **downfall**, e.g. Hamlet's inaction.

Index

Index

Further Reading

It seems like everyone has something to say about 'Hamlet', even if it's just that it's too long. Critics have been writing about it since Shakespeare's day and directors have been making films of it since... well, since cameras were invented.

Books

Reading what **someone else** has written about *Hamlet* can help you to work out what **you think** about the play. You can bring **critics** into your **essays** to **support** your argument — you **don't** need to agree with their **opinions** as long as you can say **why not**. Make sure you **reference** your critics properly too. Try some of these for size...

Samuel Johnson, *Preface to Shakespeare*, 1765

A.C. Bradley, *Shakespearean Tragedy*, Macmillan, 1904

T.S. Eliot, 'Hamlet and His Problems', in *The Sacred Wood: Essays on Poetry and Criticism*, Faber, 1920

G. Wilson Knight, *The Wheel of Fire*, Oxford University Press, 1930

Harley Granville-Barker, *Prefaces to Shakespeare*, Batsford, 1936

John Dover Wilson, *What Happens in Hamlet*, Cambridge University Press, 1935

L.C. Knights, *An Approach to Hamlet*, Chatto & Windus, 1960

Eleanor Prosser, *Hamlet and Revenge*, Stanford University Press, 1967

Elaine Showalter, 'Representing Ophelia: Women, Madness and the Responsibilities of Feminist Criticism' in Patricia Parker and Geoffrey Hartman (eds.) *Shakespeare and the Question of Theory*, Methuen, 1985

Catherine Belsey, *The Subject of Tragedy*, Methuen, 1985

Martin Coyle (ed.), *Hamlet: New Casebooks*, Macmillan, 1992

Robert N. Watson, 'Giving Up the Ghost: *Hamlet*, Revenge and Denial' in *The Rest is Silence: Death as Annihilation in the English Renaissance*, University of California Press, 1994

K. Parsons and P. Mason, *Shakespeare in Performance*, Salamander Books, 1997

Frank Kermode, *Shakespeare's Language*, Penguin/Allen Lane, 2000

Sean McEnvoy, *Shakespeare: The Basics*, Routledge, 2000

Stephen Greenblatt, *Hamlet in Purgatory*, Princeton University Press, 2001

Huw Griffiths, *Hamlet: A Reader's Guide to Essential Criticism*, Palgrave Macmillan, 2005

Films

Nothing compares to seeing a **stage production** of *Hamlet* but watching these films will help you get to grips with the **plot** and **language** of the play. It's also interesting to see how different **directors** have **interpreted** the play's **ambiguous** elements and what they've chosen to **emphasise** or **leave out**. Grab your popcorn and take a look at some of these...

Hamlet (1948): Directed by Laurence Olivier, Hamlet also played by Laurence Olivier

Hamlet (1980): Directed by Rodney Bennett, Hamlet played by Derek Jacobi

Hamlet (1990): Directed by Franco Zeffirelli, Hamlet played by Mel Gibson

The Lion King (1994): Disney animated adaptation of the *Hamlet* story

Hamlet (1996): Directed by Kenneth Branagh, Hamlet also played by Kenneth Branagh

Hamlet (2000): Directed by Michael Almereyda, Hamlet played by Ethan Hawke

Hamlet (2009): Directed by Gregory Doran, Hamlet played by David Tennant

Rosencrantz and Guildenstern Are Dead (1990): Directed by Tom Stoppard

The full version of this production is 4 hours long — if you've not got much time, there's also a version that's 2 hours long.

Who's Who in the 'Hamlet' Cartoon

You should be an expert on 'Hamlet' by now. But if you want a bit of light relief and a quick recap of the play's plot, sit yourself down and read through 'Hamlet — The Cartoon'...

Hamlet

Claudius

Gertrude

Polonius

Laertes

Ophelia

Horatio

The Ghost

Rosencrantz and Guildenstern

William Shakespeare's 'Hamlet'